Finding
THE
Career
THAT FITS YOU

Finding
THE
Career
THAT FITS YOU

Larry Burkett & Lee Ellis

Finding
THE
Career
That Fits You

The Companion Workbook to
Your Career in Changing Times

MOODY PRESS
CHICAGO

ISBN #0-8024-2522-4

5 7 9 10 8 6

Printed in the United States of America

ACKNOWLEDGMENT

Several people deserve special thanks and recognition. Beth Pinson, Deb Smith, Mike Taylor, and Bob Yarbrough gave encouragement, critique, and insights that were especially helpful.

Jim Armstrong, Peter Pace, and Sue Clark shared their creative talents; and Adeline Griffith, our editor, gave her eagle eye and professional expertise to the project.

Finally, we thank our families for their forbearance while our attention focused on writing.

CONTENTS

INTRODUCTION

If you have questions about which direction you should be going in your career, this workbook is for you; and we are confident you'll benefit from the information and exercises provided.

The concepts and tools have been developed through research and experience from working with thousands of individuals just like you. The questionnaires and surveys usually give very accurate results; yet, you can use them effectively without professional help.

There is a design to each step within the chapters and to the order of the chapters. If you skip around or don't finish some of the steps, you'll deny yourself the full benefit of the workbook. For the best result, just take your time and work from the front to the back of the book.

Chapters 1 and 2 set the stage for your thinking about work. Chapters 3 through 6 are designed to reveal your talents and occupational interests. Chapter 7 should be used to consolidate and summarize all the information from your self-assessments. The remainder of the book will help you as you apply what you've learned to your own personal life.

Each person's pattern of talents and interests will be somewhat unique. Likewise, each person has unique circumstances and needs that must be considered. That is why, ultimately, only you can make the final decision about how God has equipped you and what He has called you to do. Our prayer is that you will let Him guide you into the career that fits the design He gave you.

CHAPTER
1

FACING CAREER AND WORKPLACE ISSUES

Since you are reading this workbook, it's likely that either you or someone close to you is facing a career problem or decision. You're not alone. Career and work issues are having a major impact on the lives of millions of Americans today.

Through our experience in administering a career assessment to over 50,000 individuals, we see that the vast majority of career problems fall into one of four categories: job mismatch, no job, returning to the workforce, or young people with no direction. You probably will be able to identify with at least one of these groups. No matter which group you're in, this workbook can help you work through your career issues.

WHICH CAREER PROBLEM FITS YOUR SITUATION

1. Job mismatch—unenthusiastic, bored, stressed out

A major issue with adults continues to be job and career dissatisfaction. There are millions of people who don't like what they are doing at work. In fact, according to a recent poll, 50 percent of those surveyed said that if they were starting over they would choose a different career.[1]

When experiencing a lack of fulfillment and corresponding low motivation toward work, many people realize they did not make a good career choice. They chose a field of work that was not a good match. Many are looking for a way to find out what their talents are and what occupations might fit.

We've seen some who are stressed, even to the point of not wanting to go to work in the morning. For some, the problem of job stress is o severe they are having health problems.

One person put it this way: "I make a living at my job, but I don't look forward to going to work everyday. In fact I usually dread it, and when I'm there I look forward to five o'clock so I can go home. I wish I could make a career transition."

A person in sales said: "I can make a big sale on Friday, but I hate my job so much that I don't look forward to going to work on Monday."

2. Don't have a job—have been laid off or downsized

Mergers and cutbacks have added millions to the ranks of the unemployed—some for the first time.

"I had been with this company for 15 years and was the marketing manager for the Northeast region. Our company was bought out in a merger, and I was replaced by the guy who had a similar position with the parent company. I've been unemployed for 10 months and have no hope of a good job."

Another person said, "I worked for 'XYZ' Corporation for 12 years and thought my future was quite secure. Our company restructured, and they cut 10 percent of the management staff. I haven't been able to find employment and probably never will get back into my old field."

These cutbacks have had a tremendous impact on families. For those who have experienced downsizing, it's much like a death in the family or a divorce. As a wife whose husband is in the throes of a job search put it, "My husband's unemployment has caused tremendous stress in our family—financially, emotionally, and spiritually."

3. Entering/reentering the workforce—lacking confidence, experience, skills, and direction

This group has expanded rapidly in recent years. Some are homemakers who have decided to pursue a career now that their children are older or have left home. Others have felt the pain and hardship of divorce and now, as single parents, must go to work to provide for their families.

Entering the workforce as an adult can be a scary thought. Many who are in this position don't have any idea which direction to pursue. Others may know what they would like to do, yet they haven't kept up with the changes in their fields. Should they go to school, or should they just take entry jobs and try to get established in the workplace?

How do you gain the confidence needed to succeed at what seems like a monumental task? It comes from knowing your talents, making a commitment to develop and use them, and following a plan of action. For many in this group, just getting started at some level can give these individuals the experience and confirmation of their abilities they need to really bloom.

A lady who just received her "first full-time paycheck in sixteen years" put it this way: "When our boys reached teen age and I was ready to do something else. . .a career assessment seemed a logical place to start. I believed the Lord was directing me to. . .get back my office skills and develop my computer skills. I began to work part-time. . .at the same time going through the career assessment and counseling. I gained many skills working for the past two years, but the most important thing I gained was my self-confidence. . .to stretch myself and not to be afraid of what I don't know."

4. Young people facing the future with no career direction

The problems facing young people and their career decisions are multifaceted. First, they have had little exposure to the world of work, so they don't know much about what is available. Second, in general there is no good system in place at home, school, or church to help them make good decisions. Consequently, youth often choose an occupation out of ignorance or choose based on the current trends and values of society.

Additionally, the lack of academic motivation in students is at least partly related to their lack of a career goal. Dr. Cliff Schimmels, Christian author and educator, says that "motivation is the ability of the learner to see the applied value of the lesson to be learned."[2] If young people have no career goals and know little about work, they see no purpose for their learning. Hence, when high school students are asked the question "How was school today?", too often we hear another verse of "Boring."

Young people who go to college also suffer from a lack of career direction. Low motivation, no direction, and poorly defined career goals, such as "I want to make a lot of money," have costly consequences. Unfocused students flunk out, change majors, or flounder around, expecting one day to graduate and get a good job. Unfortunately, many who do graduate still have no idea what their talents are or what they want to do.

The waste in classroom time, lives, talent, and productivity is discouraging; and, with the rapid inflation in college costs, the expense of misdirected education and training is becoming significant.

One parent put it this way. "We educated our son through four years of college and three years of law school. He's practiced law for two years and, now, he hates it. In fact, he has quit. He says he wants to go back to school to prepare for a new career field, but we can't afford to help him anymore. When I think of all his effort and the money we invested, I could just cry."

The categories above are representative, and we know that there are others. For example, we didn't mention it, but retirement career decisions have become an important issue for many.

However, we believe that the previous illustrations are adequate to point out that career problems are widespread, and they cut across all lines of age and gender.

WHAT'S HAPPENING IN THE WORKPLACE?

We've given you some insights into the career issues people are facing. Now let's take a quick overview of the change factors that are affecting the world of work.

RAPID TECHNOLOGICAL CHANGE. New technology continues to expand at an ever increasing rate, highly impacting the way work is done. Computers are used in nearly every occupation. Robotic tools have replaced many assembly line jobs. We live in the Information Age, and the Internet has provided worldwide access to almost any information we need.

Low-cost technology has made it possible for small companies to compete with the giants. Often, speed to market determines success; and this can be to the advantage of the smaller, newer, and more flexible companies. In some cases, the new technologies enable overseas companies, where labor and raw materials may be cheaper, to operate at a better profit margin.

WORLDWIDE ECONOMIC COMPETITION. The expansion of technology has brought incredible market competition on a worldwide scale. This competition erodes profit margins, which causes companies to continually seek ways of cutting costs—of doing business more efficiently. This relentless drive to cut costs often brings drastic changes to the workplace.

REVOLUTIONARY CHANGES IN WORK STRUCTURE. Since personnel costs are usually the biggest percentage of the budget, downsizing, rightsizing, and layoffs have become a way of life. Layoffs are probably necessary to maintain a healthy economy. Through the use of technology, many industries now operate more efficiently with fewer people; and, despite the huge layoffs of the nineties, unemployment decreased. The push for corporate mergers often is related to the anticipated efficiencies from personnel reductions.

At the same time, organizational structures are being flattened so that more work is done by teams that have been empowered to carry out major projects. Projects come and go as contracts come and go; so finding a job may mean finding a new project that can utilize your talents.

The downsizing movement has given impetus for many people to leave the corporate world to start their own businesses. Entrepreneurism is growing at a rapid pace, so we can expect more small companies to spring up to provide work. But, usually, new companies also are more unstable, which adds to the insecurity in the workplace.

WHAT DOES ALL THIS MEAN TO YOU?

YOU MUST BE ABLE TO MARKET YOUR TALENTS. As you can see, the one constant is going to be change; and, if the past is an indicator, change will continue at an increasing rate. This means that you need to be flexible; you need to know your talents, interests, and passions; and you need to be able to market yourself into a job that fits you.

The word "market" may sound scary, but it just means that you have to be able to describe to someone exactly what you do very well. Even more important may be the need for you to find organizations that match your values and that have a need for someone with a passion to do what you want to do. More and more, companies are realizing how important it is to match the right person to the needs of the job. By knowing the career that fits you and by marketing yourself accordingly, you are helping employers in that talent search.

Where Is Your Job Security?

All this leads us to believe that jobs will be more transient in the future than they have been in the past. As many have found out, over the long haul you cannot look to your company for job security. We don't think there is such a thing as job security. (There is only one Source you can look to for any security in this world.) But we can assure you that the best way to increase your odds of being employed is to know your talents, develop them, and be truly excellent in your work.

Since jobs are insecure, you will have to be flexible; and that's why it's so important for you to know how to find a career that fits you. We don't like to tell people just one specific occupation in which they can excel. That will help them only until the next layoff occurs. Rather, our approach has always been to show them their pattern of talents and help them to see that their talents can be applied in a variety of settings.

As we said in the Introduction, this workbook is designed to lead you through a process that will equip you to know your God-given talents and understand how to find your calling. Our prayer is that you will place your confidence in the One who gave you your talents and be a good steward of them by being faithful to your calling.

Begin now by faithfully working your way through each chapter. We think you'll enjoy seeing how God has wonderfully equipped you for the journey on your career pathway. And in time, we trust you'll have a clear view of your calling and life purpose.

CHAPTER NOTES

1. *Wall Street Journal*/NBC poll, 1997.
2. Dr. Cliff Schimmels, *Parents' Most-Asked Questions About Kids and Schools*, Victor Books, Wheaton IL, 1989.

CHAPTER
2

GAINING A BIBLICAL
VIEW OF WORK

The main purpose of this workbook is to help you discover your talents and interests. After all, they are the keys to finding your calling and the career that fits you.

However, many people have a hard time keeping their talents in focus when they start looking for a job. That's why this chapter is designed to prepare you thoroughly with the truth that can set you free to make sound career decisions. We don't want you to get sidetracked by the temptation to pursue an occupation just because it's on someone's "hot jobs" list.

THE BEST CAREER GUIDANCE
COMES FROM BIBLICAL TRUTH

To encourage you to stick with God's principles of career planning, we will lead you through a short study to see what the Bible has to say on the subject. A thorough grounding in God's truth is your best defense against career mismatch.

Read the following verses to discover some of the truths that should guide your planning.

1. You were uniquely designed by God.

a. Psalm 119:73 says that God _____
_____
_____
_____.

b. Isaiah 44:2 says that the Lord_____
_____
_____
_____.

c. Job 10:11 says that you were_____
_____
_____
_____.

d. Psalm 139:

   verse 13 says that you were_____
_____
_____
_____.

   verse 14 says that you were_____
_____
_____
_____.

   verse 15 says that you were_____
_____
_____
_____.

2. Your talents are unique for a purpose.

a. Romans 12:4 implies that we do not all_____

_____

_____

_____

_____.

b. Romans 12:6 says that we have_____

_____

_____

_____

and that each person should _____

_____

_____

_____.

c. First Peter 4:10 says that we should_____

_____

_____

_____

_____.

d. First Corinthians 12:18-20 indicates that God has made us different because_____

_____

_____

_____.

3. To be excellent in your work, you should develop your talents.

a. Proverbs 24:27 indicates that priority should be given to_____

_____

_____.

b. Proverbs 22:29 implies that those who will have the most job security will be_____

_____

_____.

c. In the parable in Matthew 25:14-30, what does Jesus indicate that we are to do with our talents?_____

_____

_____

_____

_____.

d. Colossians 3:23 says that we are to_____

_____

_____

_____.

4. *Your vocational calling provides an important opportunity for your higher calling.*

a. Matthew 5:14 says that we are_____

_____

_____

_____

and Matthew 5:16 tells us to_____

_____

_____

_____.

b. In 2 Corinthians 5:20, the apostle Paul tells us that we are to be_____

_____

_____.

c. Colossians 3:17 indicates that we should do everything in

_____

_____

_____.

d. First Corinthians 10:31 says that the purpose of everything we do is

_____

_____

_____.

The principles you just reviewed from the Scripture provide the foundation for good career decisions. But it will take a strong commitment of faith on your part to act on them. You see, the secular world in which we live has another set of principles and priorities. They aren't written out, but they are so well accepted that, often, even some Christians never realize that God offers a better way.

If you are tempted to follow the world's priorities, stop and remember that God's way often looks foolish to the natural eye (see 1 Corinthians 2:14); but to the man or woman of faith it is the prerequisite to honoring Him and the doorway to receiving His blessings.

There are two practical implications we should draw from these biblical principles that are fundamental to good career decisions.

A. Round Pegs Fit Round Holes

We all know some version of the saying about putting a round peg in a square hole; the implication is that it doesn't work because it won't fit. That's exactly why so many people have been unable to really enjoy their work. They don't fit.

Putting the round peg in the round hole and the square peg in the square hole is the basic concept for finding a career that fits. It sounds simple, but there are two problems.

First, many people completely ignore trying to find a match. They've been told, "You can do anything if you set your mind to it," so they choose their career based on criteria other than their talents.

Second, many people don't have a clear picture of what their talents are. They may make some bad assumptions about their strengths, or they may be steered by those around them who also may not have an objective view.

This situation is addressed specifically in a recent book entitled *Boundaries* by Drs. Henry Cloud and John Townsend. Here are their comments.

> "Boundaries are where our identity comes from. Boundaries define what is me and what is not me. Our work is part of our identity because it taps into our particular giftedness and the exercise of those gifts in the community.

> "However, many people are unable to ever find a true work identity. They stumble from job to job, never really finding anything that is 'them.' More often than not, this is a boundary problem. They have not been able to own their own gifts, talents, wants, desires, and dreams because they are unable to set boundaries on others' definitions and expectations of them."[1]

B. Talents and Interests Define the Shape of Your Work Pattern

The term *boundaries* fits quite well with the concept of a pattern of talents. Boundaries define a shape, and each one of us has been given a unique shape that is determined by our talents and interests.

If you've seen the companion book to this workbook, *Your Career in Changing Times*, you may recall the simple depictions we used to illustrate the idea of a pattern of talents and how these talents match various occupations. In case you haven't seen it yet or have forgotten, they are shown below.

PATTERN FOR PERSON "A"

PERSONALITY

INTERACTING
•Optimistic
•Outgoing
SUPPORTIVE
•Understanding
•Patient

SKILLS

WORK PRIORITIES AND VALUES

VERBAL
•Counsel
•Listen
•Relate
•Encourage
•Explain

•Serve God
•Help people
•Variety

EDUCATION COUNSELING
•Counselor
•Teacher
•Personnel Manager

VOCATIONAL INTEREST

"COUNSELOR" PATTERN

PATTERN FOR PERSON "B"

PERSONALITY

CONSCIENTIOUS
•Detailed
•Accurate
STEADY
•Patient
•Consistent
•Loyal

WORK PRIORITIES AND VALUES

SKILLS

CRAFTSMAN
•Work with hands
•Repair machinery
SPATIAL
MECHANICAL

•Organization
•Neatness
•Tangible results of work

MECHANICAL
•Construction
•Electrician
•Cabinet maker
SCIENTIFIC
•Engineering

VOCATIONAL INTEREST

"CARPENTER" PATTERN

These are the patterns for two individuals and the molds for two occupations. You can see how similar Person A is to the pattern of talents and interests that are ideal for the occupation of counselor. Likewise, Person B matches the occupation of carpenter quite well. It is also obvious that Person A would not fit very well as a carpenter, and Person B probably would not be matched to the work of a counselor.

We have counseled many people who hated their work because they were in a vocational mismatch. Amazingly, no one had ever pointed out to them that they really didn't fit. When they found out their true God-given pattern, they were relieved and excited about their future work possibilities. A typical comment from our clients is, "Wow, this is so freeing. Where were you 20 years ago when I made my original career choice?"

Sadly, Life Pathways didn't exist then, but we are here now, and we are delighted to have this opportunity to share with you the concepts, process, and materials that will help you to find your calling and a career that fits you.

CHAPTER NOTES

1. Taken from the book *Boundaries* by Dr. Henry Cloud and Dr. John Townsend. Copyright © 1992 by Henry Cloud and John Townsend. Used by permission of Zondervan Publishing House.

CHAPTER
3

UNDERSTANDING YOUR PERSONALITY STRENGTHS

T he next four chapters will take you through a self-assessment that will help you to understand your talents and interests for work. In this chapter you will gain an in-depth understanding of your personality strengths and weaknesses and how they affect your vocational choices.

Before you begin, we also should point out that this chapter is the most extensive, and it will require the most work on your part. It's especially important for you to read carefully and focus your attention in order to follow the detailed instructions in the personality assessment.

Once you've completed the assessment, go back and take time to digest the concepts on personality. The questions and comments at the end of the chapter will help you to integrate what you've learned.

Ultimately, your understanding of this information will be key to your career decisions and will equip you to improve relationships in every area of your life.

Turn the page and follow the instructions to discover your personality I.D.

Life Pathways ™

Personality I.D. ™

The purpose of this instrument is educational. It is designed to help people identify their natural personality strengths. The *Personality I.D.™* is not a professional psychological instrument and should not be used to identify, diagnose, or treat psychological, mental health, and/or medical problems. Additionally, if used to evaluate personnel, the user should seek adequate legal counsel to ensure compliance with applicable local, state, and federal employment laws. The user assumes sole responsibility for any actions or decisions that are made as a result of using this aid to self-discovery. By using the *Personality I.D.* you expressly waive and relinquish any and all claims of any nature against Life Pathways, Christian Financial Concepts, any affiliated companies, and/or their employees arising out of or in connection with the use of this survey.

ISBN 1-56427-114-5

Life Pathways, PO Box 1476, Gainesville, GA 30503-1476

BEGIN HERE

INTRODUCTION

This survey booklet is not a test. There are no right or wrong answers. The results will help you gain an understanding of your basic personality profile and the characteristics shared by most people with that profile. The purpose of the *Personality I.D.*™ is educational. It is not appropriate for psychological testing. (Please read disclaimer on page 1.)

There are two surveys in this booklet. <u>Survey A is designed to reveal your natural personality profile. Survey B has two possible uses. It is available for you to evaluate the personality characteristics that are required to be successful in your current job, or it can be used by another person to reveal his or her natural personality profile.</u> You will be given more instructions on this later. The materials are organized in the following sequence: surveys, scoring, plotting of profiles, interpretations, and explanations.

BEFORE YOU TAKE THE SURVEY READ THESE CAUTIONS!

1. Personality surveys tend to be influenced by the situational focus a person has when responding. Be sure you consider the focus specified in the directions, and keep the same focus throughout the survey.

2. Avoid looking ahead or trying to analyze the survey. Just follow the step-by-step instructions.

3. This survey may look similar to others you have taken, but there are some important differences in the rating system. Be sure you understand the directions and examples.

4. By necessity, this booklet has been designed in a very linear (sequential) style, to be used by people with varying backgrounds of education and experience. If you will take the time to read and FOLLOW ALL THE DIRECTIONS step-by-step, you will be able to identify and understand your personality strengths.

Survey A
Natural Behavior

▶ **DIRECTIONS**

FOCUS: The focus for this survey is **your typical behavior.** Respond based on how you most naturally behave. Think of your core self, and answer based on your instinctive behavior, regardless of whether you consider it to be good or bad.

RESPOND: Rate each line of words from left to right on a 1, 2, 3, 4 scale <u>with 1 being the word that is least like you and 4 being the word that best describes your naturally motivated behavior.</u>

(least) 1   2   3   4 **(most)** ▷ like you

Use all ratings (1, 2, 3, 4) in each line and use each rating (1, 2, 3, 4) only once on each line. To change a response, mark through it and write the new response to the left of the box. Study the example below before starting.

Correct Example A: → |4| Enthusiastic |1| Loyal |2| Detailed |3| Commanding

Incorrect Example B: → |4| Enthusiastic |1| Loyal |3| Detailed |4| Commanding

Incorrect: Use each rating only once as in Example A.

1 is least like you ◀—— 1   2   3   4 ——▶ 4 is most like you

☐ Enthusiastic	☐ Loyal	☐ Detailed	☐ Commanding
☐ Lenient	☐ Expressive	☐ Decisive	☐ Particular
☐ Convincing	☐ Tough-Minded	☐ Meticulous	☐ Kind
☐ Independent	☐ Follow Rules	☐ Peaceful	☐ Fun-Loving
☐ High Standards	☐ Understanding	☐ People-Oriented	☐ Daring
☐ Charitable	☐ Lively	☐ Risk Taker	☐ Serious
☐ Cheerful	☐ Courageous	☐ Precise	☐ Merciful
☐ Confident	☐ Logical	☐ Supportive	☐ Inspiring
☐ Conscientious	☐ Patient	☐ Good Mixer	☐ Fearless
☐ Nonconforming	☐ Talkative	☐ Gentle	☐ Analytical
☐ Organized	☐ Assertive	☐ Popular	☐ Even-Paced
☐ Good Listener	☐ Factual	☐ Take-Charge	☐ Uninhibited
☐ Aggressive	☐ Cooperative	☐ Vibrant	☐ Accurate
☐ Efficient	☐ Direct	☐ Gracious	☐ Excitable
☐ Influencing	☐ Accommodating	☐ Focused	☐ Frank
☐ Agreeable	☐ Animated	☐ Forceful	☐ Systematic

When you have completed this survey, turn to page P-7 for further instructions.

Survey A
Scoring Key

SCORING YOUR RESULTS

Your responses from the survey have been recorded on this page. Follow the steps below to score your results.

1. Your answers are in boxes labeled AD, RI, OS, or UC. Begin with the left column and add all the numbers in the boxes labeled "AD" in each column so that you end up with an "AD" total for the entire survey. Enter this total on the line labeled "AD" at right.

2. Follow the same procedure for boxes labeled RI, OS, and UC, and enter the totals on the appropriate line at right.

3. To check for accuracy, add the totals at right for AD, RI, OS, and UC. The check total should be 160. If your check total is different, you either made an error in addition, or you may have used the same number twice on one line of the survey.

4. Finally, transfer your AD, RI, OS, and UC totals to the Survey A section at the top of page P-13.

Scoring Summary

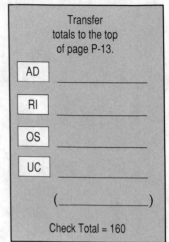

Transfer totals to the top of page P-13.

AD _____

RI _____

OS _____

UC _____

(_____)

Check Total = 160

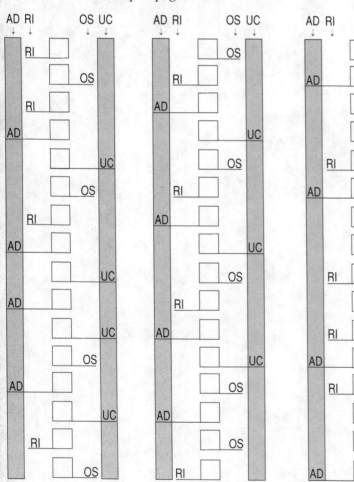

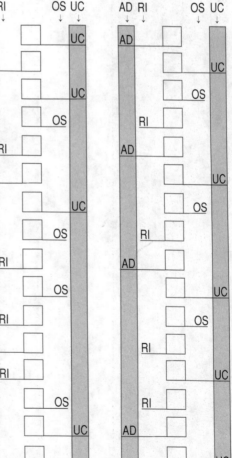

 **NEXT**

IF <u>YOU</u> PLAN TO USE SURVEY B

To compare your personality to that required in your current or recent job, turn the page and complete Survey B "Expected Work Behavior." **Survey B has a different focus,** so be sure you read the directions carefully before responding.

Turn the page ➤

OR

IF <u>YOU</u> DO NOT PLAN TO USE SURVEY B

If you choose not to use Survey B to analyze your current/recent job match, turn to page P-12 now and follow the instructions to score your Survey A.

Turn to page P-12 ➤

OR

IF <u>SOMEONE ELSE</u> WILL USE SURVEY B

Someone else (spouse, child, teenager, friend) can use Survey B to determine his or her natural personality profile. <u>In this case, be sure he or she follows the directions and focus used in Survey A for "Natural Behavior" on page P-3 and disregards those at the top of Survey B.</u>

Turn the page ➤

Survey B
Expected Work Behavior

(If this survey is being used by a second person to define natural personality, read instructions on page P-3.)

(If this survey is being used by a second person to define natural personality, read instructions on page P-3.)

> ### ▶ DIRECTIONS
>
> **FOCUS:** The focus for this survey is **your current job or most recent work situation.** Your response should be based on what your employer expects of you at work and may be quite different from your naturally motivated behavior.
>
> **RESPOND:** Rate each line of words from left to right on a 1, 2, 3, 4 scale **with 1 being the behavior least needed in your job and 4 being the behavior most needed to succeed in your job.**
>
> (least) 1   2   3   4 **(most)** ⟩ needed to succeed
>
> *Use all ratings (1, 2, 3, 4) in each line and use each rating (1, 2, 3, 4) only once on each line.* To change a response, mark through it and write the new response to the left of the box. Study the example below before starting.
>
> **Correct** Example A: → ⟦4⟧ Enthusiastic ⟦1⟧ Loyal ⟦2⟧ Detailed ⟦3⟧ Commanding
>
> **Incorrect** Example B: → ⟦4⟧ Enthusiastic ⟦1⟧ Loyal ⟦3⟧ Detailed ⟦4⟧ Commanding
>
> ⎣ *Incorrect: Use each rating only once as in Example A.* ⎦

1 is least like you ◄— 1   2   3   4 —► 4 is most like you

→	Enthusiastic	Loyal	Detailed	Commanding
→	Lenient	Expressive	Decisive	Particular
→	Convincing	Tough-Minded	Meticulous	Kind
→	Independent	Follow Rules	Peaceful	Fun-Loving
→	High Standards	Understanding	People-Oriented	Daring
→	Charitable	Lively	Risk Taker	Serious
→	Cheerful	Courageous	Precise	Merciful
→	Confident	Logical	Supportive	Inspiring
→	Conscientious	Patient	Good Mixer	Fearless
→	Nonconforming	Talkative	Gentle	Analytical
→	Organized	Assertive	Popular	Even-Paced
→	Good Listener	Factual	Take-Charge	Uninhibited
→	Aggressive	Cooperative	Vibrant	Accurate
→	Efficient	Direct	Gracious	Excitable
→	Influencing	Accommodating	Focused	Frank
→	Agreeable	Animated	Forceful	Systematic

When you have completed this survey, turn to page P-12 and continue. ▶

When you have completed this survey, turn to page P-12 and continue.

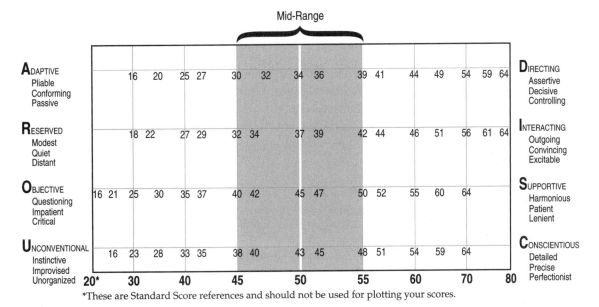

	NATURAL SURVEY A TOTALS From page P-5	
TOTAL:	A-D	_____
TOTAL:	R-I	_____
TOTAL:	O-S	_____
TOTAL:	U-C	_____

	WORK SURVEY B TOTALS From page P-11	
TOTAL:	A-D	_____
TOTAL:	R-I	_____
TOTAL:	O-S	_____
TOTAL:	U-C	_____

*These are Standard Score references and should not be used for plotting your scores.

3. Plot Your Profiles

a. Using the totals from Survey A, plot your AROU/DISC dimensions on the graph above; then connect the four points, using a straight edge. This is Graph A and reflects your natural personality profile. Refer to the example on page P-12 and note the solid line used for Graph A.

b. If you used Survey B, plot the points; then connect, using a dashed line (Graph B) or a different colored pen so you can easily see the differences between the two graphs.

c. Graph A refers to Survey A (Natural Profile), and Graph B refers to Survey B (Work Profile). If Survey B was used as a natural personality profile, use Graph A instructions and ignore number **11** on page P-29.

4. Identify Your Natural Profile

Use the points on Survey A as a guide to **check the appropriate box at right to indicate your AROU/DISC ranges.**

Survey A

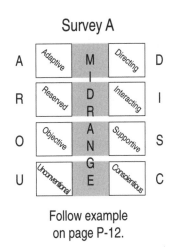

Follow example
on page P-12.

Turn the page and continue.

➤ READ THIS NEXT

UNDERSTANDING THE NEW DISC CONCEPT
OF PERSONALITY

INTRODUCTION: This personality discovery instrument is similar to the four-dimensional DISC system but rotates the graph horizontally and gives equal value to both ends of the continuum. (For example, in our new system we use the term Adaptive instead of low D.) Instead of focusing on who you are not, this instrument allows you to focus on who you are.

If you wish to compare this instrument to other personality surveys that use only the four primary dimensions of behavior, you'll notice you can still refer to the right side of the graph and locate the D, I, S, and C dimensions. Additionally, Dr. Tim LaHaye and Florence Littauer have written excellent books on temperament, using the traditional terminology for these dimensions: Choleric (D), Sanguine (I), Phlegmatic (S), and Melancholy (C). Authors Gary Smalley and John Trent use the terms Lion (D), Otter (I), Golden Retriever (S), and Beaver (C) in some of their books and presentations to describe these four dimensions.

In order to use the information in this booklet, there are several key concepts to understand.

a. We are all born with certain differences in personality and thus are motivated by different circumstances, opportunities, and environments.

b. These differences in motivation enable us to do some things better than others.

c. Different does not mean wrong; therefore, we should accept and respect those whose personalities are not like ours. It is not our role to change others.

d. All profiles/people have strengths and weaknesses. Profiles should not be used as excuses to ignore bad habits or character flaws.

e. By understanding our personalities, as well as how others are different, we are equipped to better manage our own lives and work more effectively with others.

Review the general characteristics of Adaptive-Directing, Reserved-Interacting, Objective-Supportive, Unconventional-Conscientious that follow.

The Eight Primary Patterns of Behavior

Adaptive ——————————— Directing

ADAPTIVE: People who are highly adaptive (A) are naturally motivated to be loyal and cooperative. Typically, they like to move cautiously and focus on one task at a time, but to bring stability they will adapt. They function best in an environment that will allow them to follow an established agenda and speak tactfully.

Examples:
Ruth	Ruth Graham
Timothy	President Abraham Lincoln

DIRECTING: People who are highly directive (D) are naturally motivated to control the work environment. They are usually assertive, direct, and competitive. They are typically bold and not afraid to take strong action to get the desired results. They function best in a challenging environment.

Examples:
Sarah	Barbara Walters
Paul	General George Patton

Reserved ——————————— Interacting

RESERVED: People who are highly reserved (R) are naturally motivated to be task-oriented, serious, modest, realistic, and practical. Usually they enjoy persevering in a task and many times have a dry sense of humor. They function best in an environment that will allow them to be focused and bring closure.

Examples:
Martha	President Jimmy Carter
Moses	David Brinkley

INTERACTING: People who are highly interactive (I) are naturally driven to relate to others. Usually they are verbal, friendly, outgoing, and optimistic. They are typically enthusiastic motivators and will seek out others to help them accomplish results. They function best in a friendly social environment.

Examples:
Mary Magdalene	Kathie Lee Gifford
Barnabas	President Ronald Reagan

Objective ——————————— Supportive

OBJECTIVE: People who are highly objective (O) naturally respond quickly, work at a fast pace, and like to promote change. They function best in an environment that will allow them to be active. They usually are able to be objective, cool, and detached, and they operate well in conflict.

Examples:
Daniel	Rush Limbaugh
Joshua	Sam Donaldson

SUPPORTIVE: People who are highly supportive (S) are naturally motivated to cooperate with and support others. They are usually patient, consistent, and very dependable. Being pleasant and easygoing makes them excellent team players. They function best in a supportive, harmonious environment.

Examples:
Abraham	Jackie Kennedy
Hannah	President George Bush

Unconventional ——————————— Conscientious

UNCONVENTIONAL: People who are highly unconventional (U) are naturally able to be flexible, versatile, and work with broad concepts. Typically they rely on their instincts, improvise, and operate without written procedures. They function best in an environment in which they can be spontaneous and respond quickly and candidly.

Examples:
Abigail	Joan Rivers
Peter	John Madden

CONSCIENTIOUS: People who are highly conscientious are focused on doing things right. Usually they are detail-oriented and find it easy to follow prescribed guidelines. Typically they strive for accuracy and quality and, therefore, set high standards for themselves and for others. They function best in structured environments.

Examples:
Elijah	General Omar Bradley
Luke	Albert Einstein

5. *Identify Your Strengths and Weaknesses*

The next four pages outline the typical strengths and weaknesses of the eight primary patterns of behavior. **Based on the boxes you checked on your Natural Profile from number 4, (page P-13) identify your strengths and weaknesses on each page.** If you fall in the Mid-Range, you will likely have some characteristics from each of the sections below and may find your characteristics vary, depending on the circumstances.

ADAPTIVE-DIRECTING

Instructions: If you scored in the Adaptive range, check the strengths and weaknesses in the **Adaptive Characteristics** box. If you scored in the Directing range, check the strengths and weaknesses in the **Directing Characteristics** box. If you scored in the Mid-Range, look at both the **Adaptive** and the **Directing** boxes, and check the strengths and weaknesses that apply to you.

ADAPTIVE CHARACTERISTICS

OVERVIEW: Adaptive personalities are motivated to accept the environment, rather than control it.

CHECK ALL THE STRENGTHS AND WEAKNESSES THAT APPLY TO YOU.

TYPICAL STRENGTHS		TYPICAL WEAKNESSES

TYPICAL STRENGTHS		TYPICAL WEAKNESSES	
____ Gentle	____ Sensitive	____ Unassertive	____ Timid
____ Tactful	____ Process-Oriented	____ Too Sensitive	____ Become Resentful
____ Adaptable	____ Lenient	____ Underestimate Self	____ Lack Confidence
____ Easygoing	____ Mild	____ Don't Take a Stand	____ Slow to Confront
____ Cautious	____ Cooperative	____ Shy	____ Dependent

MID-RANGE ADAPTIVE-DIRECTING

NOTE: If you scored in the Mid-Range, look at both the **Adaptive** and **Directing** boxes, and check the strengths and weaknesses that apply to you.

DIRECTING CHARACTERISTICS

OVERVIEW: Directing personalities are naturally motivated to be in control of their environment.

CHECK ALL THE STRENGTHS AND WEAKNESSES THAT APPLY TO YOU.

TYPICAL STRENGTHS		TYPICAL WEAKNESSES	
____ Bold	____ Assertive	____ Impatient	____ Impulsive
____ Direct	____ Results-Oriented	____ Insensitive	____ Too Blunt
____ Confident	____ Independent	____ Dislike Details	____ Hate Routines
____ Competitive	____ Like Challenges	____ Poor Listener	____ Self-Centered
____ Pioneering	____ Visionary	____ Demanding	____ Controlling

RESERVED-INTERACTING

Instructions: If you scored in the Reserved range, check the strengths and weaknesses in the **Reserved Characteristics** box. If you scored in the Interacting range, check the strengths and weaknesses in the **Interacting Characteristics** box. If you scored in the Mid-Range, look at both the **Reserved** and the **Interacting** boxes, and check the strengths and weaknesses that apply to you.

RESERVED CHARACTERISTICS

OVERVIEW: Reserved personalities are able to work well alone and are energized by reflective thought, rather than extensive social activity.

CHECK ALL THE STRENGTHS AND WEAKNESSES THAT APPLY TO YOU.

TYPICAL STRENGTHS

- ____ Work Well Alone
- ____ Focused
- ____ Realistic
- ____ Earnest
- ____ Factual
- ____ Reserved
- ____ Efficient
- ____ Frugal
- ____ Dry Humor
- ____ Don't Exaggerate

TYPICAL WEAKNESSES

- ____ Appear Unfriendly
- ____ Secretive
- ____ Shy in Public
- ____ Pessimistic
- ____ Don't Share Ideas
- ____ Can Be Curt
- ____ Not Transparent
- ____ Tire from Socializing
- ____ Lack Enthusiasm
- ____ Quietly Self-Righteous

MID-RANGE RESERVED-INTERACTING

NOTE: If you scored in the Mid-Range, look at both the **Reserved** and **Interacting** boxes, and check the strengths and weaknesses that apply to you.

INTERACTING CHARACTERISTICS

OVERVIEW: Interacting personalities are naturally motivated to relate to others through verbal communication. They are energized by people interaction.

CHECK ALL THE STRENGTHS AND WEAKNESSES THAT APPLY TO YOU.

TYPICAL STRENGTHS

- ____ Outgoing
- ____ Good Talker
- ____ Entertaining
- ____ Lively
- ____ Optimistic
- ____ Good First Impression
- ____ Persuasive
- ____ Fun-Loving
- ____ Enthusiastic
- ____ Inspiring

TYPICAL WEAKNESSES

- ____ Talk Too Much
- ____ Disorganized
- ____ Poor Money Manager
- ____ Try to Impress Others
- ____ Get Too Emotional
- ____ Not Time Sensitive
- ____ Overlook Key Details
- ____ Too Optimistic
- ____ Get Overcommitted
- ____ Exaggerate

Turn the page and continue.

OBJECTIVE-SUPPORTIVE

Instructions: If you scored in the Objective range, check the strengths and weaknesses in the **Objective Characteristics** box. If you scored in the Supportive range, check the strengths and weaknesses in the **Supportive Characteristics** box. If you scored in the Mid-Range, look at both the **Objective** and the **Supportive** boxes, and check the strengths and weaknesses that apply to you.

OBJECTIVE CHARACTERISTICS

OVERVIEW: Objective personalities are motivated to action and prefer frequent changes in the environment.

CHECK ALL THE STRENGTHS AND WEAKNESSES THAT APPLY TO YOU.

TYPICAL STRENGTHS

____ Action-Oriented	____ Initiating		
____ Energetic	____ Dynamic		
____ Spontaneous	____ Flexible		
____ Change-Oriented	____ Want Variety		
____ Alert	____ Quick to React		

TYPICAL WEAKNESSES

____ Too Impatient	____ Not Content		
____ Neglect Commitments	____ Abrupt		
____ Can't Be Still	____ Hyperactive		
____ Easily Distracted	____ Don't Finish Projects		
____ Insensitive	____ Too Critical		

MID-RANGE OBJECTIVE-SUPPORTIVE

NOTE: If you scored in the Mid-Range, look at both the **Objective** and **Supportive** boxes, and check the strengths and weaknesses that apply to you.

SUPPORTIVE CHARACTERISTICS

OVERVIEW: Supportive personalities are naturally motivated to maintain stability and harmony in the environment by cooperating with others.

CHECK ALL THE STRENGTHS AND WEAKNESSES THAT APPLY TO YOU.

TYPICAL STRENGTHS

____ Harmonious	____ Peaceful		
____ Good Listener	____ Considerate		
____ Cooperative	____ Understanding		
____ Patient	____ Steady		
____ Supportive	____ Loyal		

TYPICAL WEAKNESSES

____ Compromise Too Much	____ Vacillate		
____ Don't Like Change	____ Get in a Rut		
____ Too Trusting	____ Naive		
____ Afraid to Confront	____ Noncommittal		
____ Too Sensitive	____ Passive		

UNCONVENTIONAL-CONSCIENTIOUS

Instructions: If you scored in the Unconventional range, check the strengths and weaknesses in the **Unconventional Characteristics** box. If you scored in the Conscientious range, check the strengths and weaknesses in the **Conscientious Characteristics** box. If you scored in the Mid-Range, look at both the **Unconventional** and the **Conscientious** boxes, and check the strengths and weaknesses that apply to you.

UNCONVENTIONAL CHARACTERISTICS

OVERVIEW: Unconventional personalities are motivated by the opportunity to use their own style to react on the spot without extensive preparation.

CHECK ALL THE STRENGTHS AND WEAKNESSES THAT APPLY TO YOU.

TYPICAL STRENGTHS

____ Independent	____ Confident		
____ Unconventional	____ Free-Spirited		
____ Versatile	____ Generalist		
____ Pragmatic	____ Good Estimator		
____ Respond Quickly	____ Good at Impromptu		

TYPICAL WEAKNESSES

____ Disorganized	____ Unprepared
____ Unfocused	____ Overlook Details
____ Opinionated	____ Rebellious
____ Undisciplined	____ Ignore Rules
____ Careless	____ Messy

MID-RANGE UNCONVENTIONAL-CONSCIENTIOUS

NOTE: If you scored in the Mid-Range, look at both the **Unconventional** and **Conscientious** boxes, and check the strengths and weaknesses that apply to you.

CONSCIENTIOUS CHARACTERISTICS

OVERVIEW: Conscientious personalities are naturally motivated to prepare thoroughly in order to achieve a high standard of quality in everything undertaken.

CHECK ALL THE STRENGTHS AND WEAKNESSES THAT APPLY TO YOU.

TYPICAL STRENGTHS

____ Accurate	____ Thorough
____ Organized	____ Analytical
____ Cautious	____ Like to Be Prepared
____ Conscientious	____ High Standards
____ Detailed	____ Focused

TYPICAL WEAKNESSES

____ Too Picky	____ Unrealistic Standards
____ Too Sensitive	____ Internalize Emotions
____ Too Cautious	____ Perfectionist
____ Cold	____ Overly Analytical
____ Rigid	____ Too Inflexible

Turn the page and continue.

6. List Your Key Strengths

Look back at the strengths you marked on the previous four pages and identify the seven behaviors that represent your strongest personality talents. List these key strengths below. Space also has been provided for your comments on how these could be used in your work.

Remember, strengths are behaviors that come so easily it's hard not to use them because it's the way you're naturally motivated to act.

Strengths   **Comments**

1. _____   _____

2. _____   _____

3. _____   _____

4. _____   _____

5. _____   _____

6. _____   _____

7. _____   _____

The opportunity to use these strengths should be a major consideration in any career decision.

COMMENT: Many people are discouraged in their work because they are not operating from their natural strengths. Solving this one problem can make a tremendous difference in both effectiveness and contentment in the workplace.

CAUTION: Keep in mind that a strength overdone can be a major weakness. For example, being a gifted communicator can be an important talent for anyone whose job is to influence others. But a communicator who talks too much or constantly gets off the subject or is insensitive to listeners has a serious weakness.

7. List Your Key Weaknesses

Review the weaknesses you marked on the previous pages. In the spaces below, list the seven most prominent problem areas in your personality profile. You may want to consider how these weaknesses might affect you at work and add your comments.

Weaknesses   **Comments**

1. _____   _____

2. _____   _____

3. _____   _____

4. _____   _____

5. _____   _____

6. _____   _____

7. _____   _____

DEALING WITH YOUR WEAK AREAS

Everyone has weaknesses. By recognizing your weak areas, then correcting them or working around them, you can improve your performance. Generally, your career choices should minimize the exposure of your weaknesses. For example, if you are Adaptive and have the typical limitations of that profile, you would want to avoid cold-call selling, especially where there is face-to-face rejection. This type of work usually requires strengths that are not natural to the Adaptive profile.

Keep in mind, however, that we all have to do some things in our work that don't come naturally. Through a mature attitude and a dedication to excellence, we usually can persevere in those areas. Since we cannot totally avoid operating in areas where we are not naturally talented, it is important to have some self-improvement programs.

For example, almost every job increasingly requires a higher degree of communicative skills. If you have problems expressing yourself, it would be a good idea to take a public speaking course. If you can't write a good paragraph, read more and then work on your writing skills. At the same time, if you're not a strong communicator, you probably would want to avoid occupations in which communications are a key part of the job.

Keep in mind, the goal is to maximize the use of your strengths and still deal effectively with your weaknesses.

CAUTION: It is not acceptable to use your personality profile as a way to justify irresponsible or unkind behavior or attitudes. We all have some real problem areas in our personalities. Look at your list of weaknesses and pray for changes in any areas of your behavior that need to be improved.

8. Confirmation and Use of Your Profile Information

After you have completed numbers *6* and *7*, ask someone who knows you well to review your list of strengths and weaknesses. You may need objective insights to confirm the results. Focus his or her input on areas in which you have questions. Your goal is to identify your key strengths and weaknesses and then use that information as you plan your career and personal growth.

Your list of strengths and weaknesses provides a powerful insight into your personality style. Use this information as you evaluate various occupations to see if they match your abilities. If you are already in a career field, you may be able to adapt your duties to fit your strengths. If you are a manager, you should consider selecting your staff to cover your limitations. Also look at your employees' strengths to see how well they match their responsibilities.

Remember, since each of us is different, we will have different strengths. Be thankful for yours, but don't expect others to be exactly like you. By knowing your strengths and operating from them, you'll maximize your effectiveness.

Turn the page and continue.

9. Identify Your Blended Profile

Thus far you have looked only at the pure A-D, R-I, O-S, and U-C characteristics. In reality, most people have a blend of these dimensions that affects their behavior. Your blended profile is defined by Graph A, so refer to page P-13 and then compare Graph A to the 17 graphs shown at right. Identify the blended profile graph that most closely matches the dimensions of your graph. Note: If all four of your scores fall into or very near the balanced region of the graph on page P-13, see Transition Profile on page P-29.

List your blended profile here _____, (___).
name   number

Illustration. Our original example on page P-12 had a Graph A that was Adaptive, Mid-Range, Supportive, Conscientious. Someone with this graph would identify with profile number 12 "Detailist." (Note the graph on page P-12 has a mid-range score on the R-I dimension and would therefore be more outgoing than the typical blended profile description of a detailist shown on page P-27.)

It is also important to read over profiles that are similar to yours. For example, someone with a "Detailist" pattern, should also review other Supportive and Conscientious profiles, such as "Researcher" (13), "Cautious Thinker" (15), and perhaps even "Supporter" (10).

List two or three blended profiles that have graphs similar to yours.

_____, (___); _____, (___); _____, (___).
name   number   name   number   name   number

10. Confirm Your Blended Profile

Compare your blended profile description (see pages P-24 to P-29) to what you think your typical behaviors are. It's likely you will be able to identify with most of the statements. Underline the areas that clearly seem to fit you.

Also look at the other profiles you listed above that are very similar to yours and underline any of the descriptions that apply.

Occasionally, an individual will realize that a similar profile actually matches better overall than the one revealed in the survey. For instance, after examining both profiles, someone who comes out with a "Detailist" profile may realize that he or she really is more of a "Researcher." This is not a conflict but a refinement of what you need to know: the elements of your personality and how they affect your work.

After you have confirmed areas that apply to you, you may want to write out the information you have underlined in the same format in which the profiles are given. This information will serve as important criteria for evaluating various career options.

There is one final step needed to complete the confirmation of your blended profile. Ask someone who knows you well to review the profile and tell you if he or she sees you the way you see yourself. Honest feedback will help you to refine your profile and confirm the information you have learned in the *Personality I.D.*

17 Blended Profiles

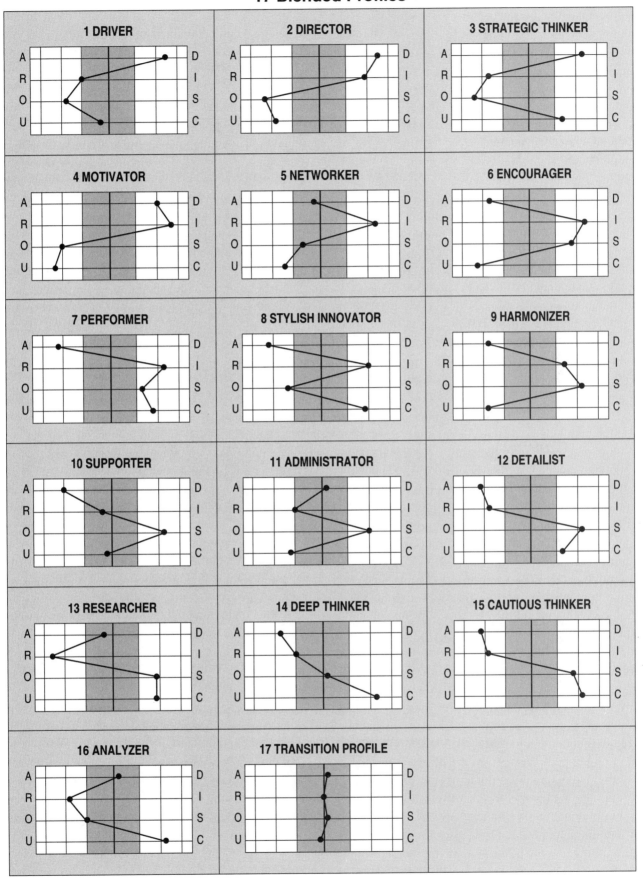

1 DRIVER

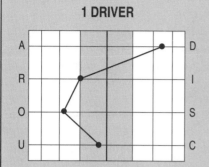

1. **Contribution to Work:** Drivers are result-oriented individualists who excel at seeing the "big picture." They take charge, define goals, and create pressure to get results.

2. **Work Environment:** They function most effectively when given independence, challenge, obstacles to overcome, and problems to be solved.

3. **Task/People Orientation:** For Drivers, the priority rests with the task. As a result, relationships definitely become secondary to meeting the goal.

4. **Mobility Factor:** These people like to be active, constantly seeking new challenges. They flourish when they have variety and are free from detail and confining routines.

5. **Stress:** Stress is created for Drivers when they are unable to control their work environment, particularly when it lacks direction, purpose, and goals. Routines and extensive detail work heighten their anxiety.

6. **Performance Improvement:** Drivers should recognize the need for the teamwork required to meet their goals. More patience and appreciation for workers as people rather than as components of a plan will help.

7. **Leadership:** They assume authority, define goals, and delegate tasks. They are daring pioneers who are masters of holding others accountable for producing results.

2 DIRECTOR

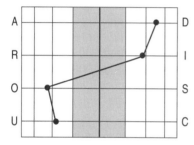

1. **Contribution to Work:** Directors easily grasp the "big picture" and use verbal skills and high energy to mobilize people and get results. They welcome a challenge, especially the opportunity to create something new.

2. **Work Environment:** These people enjoy challenge, variety, and the opportunity to influence and inspire others. They strive for prestige and recognition.

3. **Task/People Orientation:** Directors relate well with people but, under pressure, will give priority to the task.

4. **Mobility Factor:** They need mobility and want to be engaged in multiple projects. They seek a constant flurry of activity, variety, and change.

5. **Stress:** The confinement of routines, processing detailed information, and lack of access to people create stress for Directors. They tend to over-commit their time and cause stress to themselves and others.

6. **Performance Improvement:** Directors should temper their expectations and optimism with realistic views of the amount of work required to obtain goals.

7. **Leadership:** These leaders define the goal and then motivate others to work together to accomplish it.

3 STRATEGIC THINKER

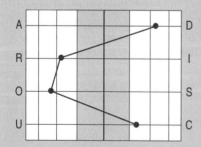

1. **Contribution to Work:** Strategic Thinkers are visionaries who synthesize facts, events, and concepts in order to develop long-range plans. They improve efficiency and get results by initiating change within the organization.

2. **Work Environment:** Strategic Thinkers are independent and creative thinkers. They enjoy defining goals and procedures.

3. **Task/People Orientation:** Since they are primarily task-oriented, they enjoy working alone.

4. **Mobility Factor:** They prefer a mixture of mobile and stationary duties. They will focus on detailed, precise information for a short time in order to achieve the goal.

5. **Stress:** Stress is created for Strategic Thinkers when they are unable to control the quality and direction of their work environment. Routines and disorganization also cause stress.

6. **Performance Improvement:** Strategic Thinkers should become more aware of the total effort required to carry out their ideas and plans. Developing team awareness and seeking feedback from key staff is important.

7. **Leadership:** These leaders develop the "big picture" and the long-range plans to achieve it. They communicate the vision, initiate change by designing new systems, and use their cautious natures to keep quality high.

4 MOTIVATOR

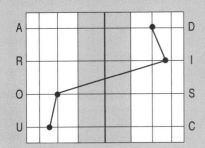

1. **Contribution to Work:** Motivators use strong communication skills and enthusiasm to sell, convince, or motivate people toward a goal.

2. **Work Environment:** They are people-oriented. They enjoy variety, recognition, prestige, and minimal detail work.

3. **Task/People Orientation:** Motivators strike a keen balance between commitment to people and tasks, making them effective leaders.

4. **Mobility Factor:** They need mobility. Their high energy levels seek an outlet through variety, changes, and quick closure on goals.

5. **Stress:** Motivators are stressed by details and routine tasks. The lack of rapid progress or access to people also creates stress.

6. **Performance Improvement:** They should use more caution and become less impulsive. Learning to say "no" and controlling optimism help Motivators to be more effective.

7. **Leadership:** These leaders define goals, then offer enthusiasm and exhortation to motivate others to achieve results. However, Motivators need to be aware that because of their strong personalities people around them sometimes feel used or manipulated.

5 NETWORKER

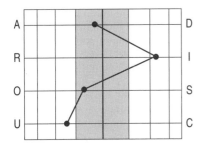

1. **Contribution to Work:** Networkers influence people through friendship, enthusiasm, humor, and strong communication skills. They seem to know everyone and network easily.

2. **Work Environment:** They seek a work setting offering the opportunity to influence, entertain, and impress people. Networkers like to express creative ideas and have freedom from routine and details.

3. **Task/People Orientation:** Networkers are people-persons who may become so totally engrossed in communicating that they sometimes lose focus on the task.

4. **Mobility Factor:** These persons must have activity, change, and variety, or they become bored.

5. **Stress:** Networkers are stressed by detail work, isolation from people, and being confined to a desk. They tend to procrastinate and then get stressed out with deadlines.

6. **Performance Improvement:** They should prioritize tasks and focus on timely completion by avoiding distractions from new ideas, projects, and opportunities. They need more facts and details to temper their optimism.

7. **Leadership:** Networkers lead by being in the spotlight and selling the vision or product with high energy, talk, humor, and enthusiasm.

6 ENCOURAGER

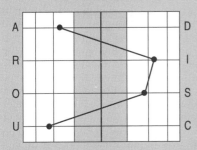

1. **Contribution to Work:** Encouragers use strong interpersonal skills to project concern and compassion. They offer faithfulness and dependability to those in need. As excellent mediators, they promote harmony within the group.

2. **Work Environment:** They seek the opportunity to encourage, develop, and nurture people. Naturally spontaneous, they prefer to be free from rigid deadlines or details. They work best in a harmonious environment and benefit from structure.

3. **Task/People Orientation:** Their commitment to helping others solve problems takes priority over other tasks.

4. **Mobility Factor:** Encouragers enjoy variety in their schedules. They prefer relating to many different people.

5. **Stress:** These persons are stressed by unresolved conflict, pressure to take charge of others, and deadlines that cause them to compromise relationships

6. **Performance Improvement:** They should realize that people are helped when projects are completed accurately and on time.

7. **Leadership:** They build lasting friendships with people through mediating, caring, and showing genuine concern.

Turn the page and continue.

7 PERFORMER

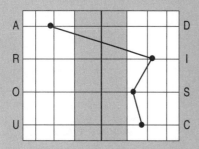

1. **Contribution to Work:** Performers enjoy using creative ideas and information in order to energize, influence, or entertain people.

2. **Work Environment:** They seek a variety in work that includes time alone for preparation, and time with people in order to use their strong interpersonal skills.

3. **Task/People Orientation:** They want people interaction but will focus on thorough task preparation. A balance between preparation and presentation is best.

4. **Mobility Factor:** They require mobility to allow for people involvement and expression of their high energy level. They want flurries of activity, interspersed with periods of methodical research and preparation.

5. **Stress:** Performers experience stress when they are cut off from people and/or adequate time for reflection and preparation. They are stressed by having to make decisions that may bring the disapproval of others.

6. **Performance Improvement:** They need to bring focus to their work by tempering their new ideas, slowing down, and being disciplined to finish tasks on time.

7. **Leadership:** They lead with strong verbal abilities and enthusiasm, and by building group consensus, influencing through a mastery of precise information.

8 STYLISH INNOVATOR

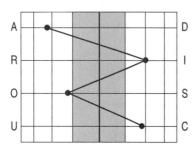

1. **Contribution to Work:** Innovators excel at generating new ideas that have an appealing flair. They use enthusiastic communication skills and extensive knowledge to influence others.

2. **Work Environment:** Although they are "people-persons," they do need time alone to research and organize their facts. Opportunities "to discover and tell" the latest information give satisfaction.

3. **Task/People Orientation:** They are primarily committed to influencing people. However, they are willing to work alone in order to ensure accuracy in what they say to others.

4. **Mobility Factor:** Mobility is needed as an outlet for their high energy level. They tend to have flurries of activity, interspersed with periods of methodical research and preparation.

5. **Stress:** They are stressed by extended periods of working alone, carrying sole responsibility for directing major projects and overcommitment to multiple projects. Lack of recognition compounds their frustrations.

6. **Performance Improvement:** They should subdue impulsive actions, slow down, and focus on how the new idea or project relates to the overall goal.

7. **Leadership:** Stylish Innovators lead by communicating the latest information, impressive facts, and data in a way that generates excitement, enthusiasm, and respect.

9 HARMONIZER

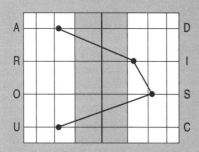

1. **Contribution to Work:** Harmonizers offer pleasant, positive attitudes and work cooperatively to complete tasks. They are good listeners with good team-building skills.

2. **Work Environment:** They desire freedom from conflict, along with opportunities to encourage, support, and assist others. They need frequent feedback from those who provide accountability.

3. **Task/People Orientation:** Their priorities rest with maintaining harmony and preserving relationships with people. As such, they may compromise the task to avoid confrontation.

4. **Mobility Factor:** Harmonizers seek balance between stability and moderate change in daily scheduling. They will need some mobility in order to relate to people.

5. **Stress:** Stress comes from unresolved conflict or when others are upset and angry with them. Too many projects and enmeshment with the personal problems of others create anxiety.

6. **Performance Improvement:** Harmonizers need to be more assertive by learning to say "no." Holding others accountable, when appropriate, would improve their effectiveness.

7. **Leadership:** They lead by building good relations and conveying care and compassion for others.

10 SUPPORTER

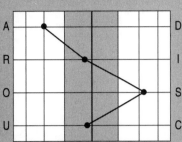

1. **Contribution to Work:** Supporters bring steadiness, consistency, and loyalty to their work. They have excellent abilities to follow through and complete tasks.

2. **Work Environment:** They seek harmony in relationships, a considerate employer, and a consistent pace, unencumbered by interruptions and changes.

3. **Task/People Orientation:** These persons are good with both tasks and people. They excel at supporting others by carrying out routine tasks.

4. **Mobility Factor:** Supporters seek steadiness, regularity, and consistency in their work. They need a daily routine and minimum overnight travel.

5. **Stress:** They are stressed by conflict, unexpected changes, lack of appreciation, and chaotic or unpredictable work settings.

6. **Performance Improvement:** Supporters need to accept some conflict as necessary to the work process. They will increase their value by expressing honest differences and/or perceptions. Accepting change as a natural occurrence will improve their effectiveness.

7. **Leadership:** They lead by setting the example. They are very dependable in carrying out their responsibilities and are very loyal.

11 ADMINISTRATOR

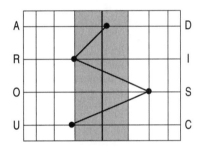

1. **Contribution to Work:** Administrators are very persistent and determined in reaching their goals. They are also strong on follow-through and good at managing details.

2. **Work Environment:** Administrators like predictability and regularity. They work best in a structured environment with clearly defined goals and the freedom to exercise authority.

3. **Task/People Orientation:** They are primarily task-oriented but relate well to people.

4. **Mobility Factor:** They have no problem working in one place for an extended period of time and are able to stay focused on one project.

5. **Stress:** Administrators are stressed by people who block their goals. Confrontational people, know-it-alls, and those who talk too much or pry into their private lives also cause stress.

6. **Performance Improvement:** They need to avoid being too sensitive, accept constructive criticisms, and keep work in balance with other areas of life.

7. **Leadership:** Administrators lead by setting the example and achieving goals. Their strong work ethic encourages others to excel. Administrators have an excellent ability to deal calmly and directly with people.

12 DETAILIST

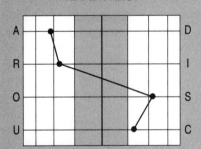

1. **Contribution to Work:** Detailists, as the name would imply, are very good with details. They are organized, thorough, and strive for accuracy.

2. **Work Environment:** They function best in structured environments with established goals and procedures. Detailists want to be thoroughly trained for all assignments, and they need companies/organizations that value the highest standards of integrity.

3. **Task/People Orientation:** Detailists are primarily task-oriented and do not want to be interrupted. They are good listeners and can provide well-thought-out counsel to others.

4. **Mobility Factor:** They can stay focused and in one location for long periods of time, do not want too much variety, and prefer to specialize.

5. **Stress:** Detailists are stressed by changes without time to prepare, disorganization, disruptions to their schedule, and conflict.

6. **Performance Improvement:** They may need to act on the results of their preliminary analysis and research. They should remember that they won't always be able to have all the answers before making decisions, and they should keep the big picture in mind.

7. **Leadership:** Detailists lead by planning, organizing, scheduling, and monitoring details. They communicate a sense of integrity and follow high standards.

Turn the page and continue. ➤

13 RESEARCHER

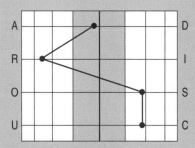

1. **Contribution to Work:** Researchers are very efficient and accurate with detail work. They are strong enough to stand up to others who try to divert their efforts.

2. **Work Environment:** They like to work where they are not bothered by small talk or interruptions. They enjoy working alone on projects and prefer written communications over conversation.

3. **Task/People Orientation:** Researchers are very task-driven and results-oriented. Interactions with people are usually short and direct.

4. **Mobility Factor:** This group is very good at remaining still and working on one project for long periods of time.

5. **Stress:** Researchers are so pro-ductivity-oriented that interruptions, office politics, and talkers usually stress them. They also notice co-workers who don't pull their share of the load. They don't seek the spotlight for their achievements but are stressed when they don't get credit.

6. **Performance Improvement:** They need to relax a little and keep a good balance in life and work.

7. **Leadership:** Researchers lead by being productive, by keeping the activity moving in a timely fashion, and by being direct with those who are falling behind.

14 DEEP THINKER

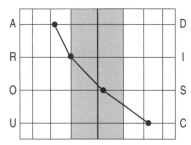

1. **Contribution to Work:** Deep Thinkers are conscientious about their work. Because of their persistent search for truth, they focus keenly on the meaning and purpose of life and work.

2. **Work Environment:** They like a dependable, well-organized work structure where accuracy, truth, and logic are valued.

3. **Task/People Orientation:** Deep Thinkers are primarily concept- and task-oriented. To understand why things are the way they are and how they should be, they like time to think through ideas and problems.

4. **Mobility Factor:** Deep Thinkers are able to remain still for long periods of time as they ponder the issues at hand.

5. **Stress:** Changes without knowing why and not being included in the planning process cause stress. Having to perform without time to thoroughly prepare creates anxiety.

6. **Performance Improvement:** They should look for opportunities to move ahead with a good solution rather than wait for the ideal solution. Deep Thinkers need to reach out to others and develop a network.

7. **Leadership:** They tend to be polite, but reserved, preferring to monitor facts and data to keep things on track. They may work a key project themselves in order to be sure it's done right.

15 CAUTIOUS THINKER

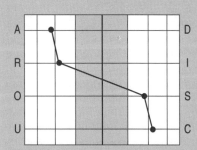

1. **Contribution to Work:** Cautious Thinkers seek to be logical in everything they do. They are motivated to be accurate, practical, and thorough.

2. **Work Environment:** They enjoy work that is organized, structured, and even-paced. They need clearly defined goals, time to think, and leadership that values truth and accuracy.

3. **Task/People Orientation:** Cautious Thinkers are task-oriented. They prefer working with data, knowledge, or things more than people. They like to work alone so they can work uninterrupted.

4. **Mobility Factor:** Cautious Thinkers can stay in one place for an extended period of time in order to keep focused. They prefer to complete one project before starting another.

5. **Stress:** Both emotional displays by others and changes without time to prepare cause them stress. Disorganization and a lack of logic also frustrate this group.

6. **Performance Improvement:** Cautious Thinkers need to step out into new areas, take more calculated risks, and remember that everything does not have to be done to perfection.

7. **Leadership:** They lead by planning, organizing, and using structure and procedures to manage.

16 ANALYZER

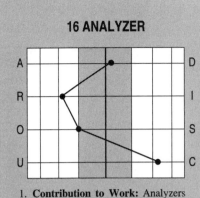

1. **Contribution to Work:** Analyzers are natural organizers and administrators. They are good at analyzing facts and working details.

Accuracy is a strength.

2. **Work Environment:** They want to be structured but with challenges and problems to analyze and some variety. They like to communicate by teaching, managing, or advising.

3. **Task/People Orientation:** Primarily task-oriented, Analyzers also are drawn to people by a secondary drive to produce results by directing others.

4. **Mobility Factor:** Their primary need is to be stationary and focused on one problem. They also have a need to move about and have variety.

5. **Stress:** Analyzers are stressed by being pushed in a direction that violates their basic motivation toward logic, truth, or efficiency. Not having time to process information and to plan also creates stress.

6. **Performance Improvement:** They need to reduce the drive to overanalyze and move ahead with action steps.

7. **Leadership:** They lead by organizing, delegating, and explaining in their area of expertise. They usually have the facts and are good at keeping the work efforts focused.

---

17 TRANSITION PROFILE

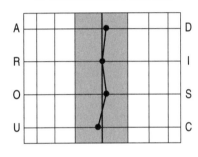

On occasion, a person's profile comes out with all scores in the gray area.

This pattern typically indicates that the individual is undergoing some significant life transitions that are confusing his or her self-concept.

There are a number of factors and life circumstances that can mask one's perception of self and how he or she naturally responds to various environments. These include an unplanned change in occupation, unemployment, a divorce, recurrent family problems, a change in mental or physical health, or some similar circumstance.

Having a transition pattern is not a cause for alarm, but it can be an indication of stress. The individual should consider seeking counsel from a spouse, pastor, close friend, or professional who is able to identify and deal with any stresses that are occurring.

The passing of time usually results in a clearer personality profile. We recommend retaking the survey in 60 to 90 days when circumstances have changed.

---

11. *Compare Your Work Requirements to Your Natural Strengths*

The graph you developed on page P-13 from Survey B describes the way you think you should be operating in your work. If there is a significant difference between Graph A and Graph B in points (two or more blocks in any of the dimensions), you probably are experiencing some stress in that area of your work. The greater the divergence, the more stress you are likely to experience.

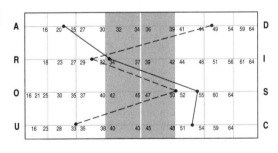

For instance, in the example at left the A-D dimension of Graph A shows the **natural** behavior in the Adaptive dimension (21), but the work Graph B shows the **expected** behavior to be in the Directing dimension (47). Our example apparently is having to stretch his or her behavior to be more dominant, direct, and bold than is natural. Such a behavioral stretch requires a large expenditure of energy and can cause frustration, anxiety, and job stress.

Also, note that the U-C dimension of Graphs A and B are separated by three blocks. Our example is having to be less conscientious and detailed and more independent and unstructured than is natural. Over a period of time a mismatch like this (person to the job) can cause significant job stress.

Go back to page P-13 and compare your Graph A with Graph B. If the A-D, R-I, O-S, and U-C points are relatively close for the two graphs (less than two blocks), then your work requires behaviors that are reasonably compatible with your personality. If this is the case, you may skip the next page.

If Graphs A and B points are significantly separated (two or more blocks) for any dimension of A-D, R-I, O-S, or U-C, you may be experiencing work stress from having to exhibit behaviors that do not come naturally.

Turn the page and continue.

12. *Analyze Graph A/Graph B Differences*

If there is a significant difference (two or more blocks) in your graph points on page 13, check the applicable diagrams below and use them to help you analyze potential stress areas.

A-D Dimension

Adaptive —— A ——|—— B —— Directing

IF YOUR GRAPH A SCORE IS MORE ADAPTIVE AND YOUR GRAPH B SCORE IS MORE DIRECTING. You are probably having to be more dominant and directive than is normal for you. Consider establishing a formal structure and reorganizing your staff to reduce the amount of directing you have to do.

Adaptive —— B ——|—— A —— Directing

IF YOUR GRAPH A SCORE IS MORE DIRECTING AND YOUR GRAPH B SCORE IS MORE ADAPTIVE. You may be impatient and frustrated by a lack of control over the methods, procedures, or results of your work. More opportunity to take responsibility for doing things your way to get results would reduce stress.

R-I Dimension

Reserved —— A ——|—— B —— Interacting

IF YOUR GRAPH A SCORE IS MORE RESERVED AND GRAPH B IS MORE INTERACTING. You are having to be more extroverted than is normal. Having to constantly meet new people is probably taking energy from you. More solitary tasks at work would relieve some stress.

Reserved —— B ——|—— A —— Interacting

IF YOUR GRAPH A SCORE IS MORE INTERACTING AND GRAPH B IS MORE RESERVED. You are probably not getting enough social interaction in your duties at work and would function more effectively at tasks where you have more opportunity to influence people.

O-S Dimension

Objective —— A ——|—— B —— Supportive

IF YOUR GRAPH A SCORE IS MORE OBJECTIVE AND GRAPH B IS MORE SUPPORTIVE. You are probably feeling stress from a lack of variety and change in your work. Frequent changes in your tasks, more new challenges, and increased physical activity would reduce stress.

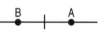

Objective —— B ——|—— A —— Supportive

IF YOUR GRAPH A SCORE IS MORE SUPPORTIVE AND YOUR GRAPH B IS MORE OBJECTIVE. You may be experiencing too much conflict, too much change, or too fast a pace at work. More harmony and stability would reduce your stress at work.

U-C Dimension

Unconventional —— A ——|—— B —— Conscientious

IF YOUR GRAPH A SCORE IS MORE UNCONVENTIONAL AND GRAPH B IS MORE CONSCIENTIOUS. Your work requires more attention to detail and depth than is natural for you. More independence, less structure, and the opportunity to work from the big-picture perspective will reduce stress.

Unconventional —— B ——|—— A —— Conscientious

IF YOUR GRAPH A SCORE IS MORE CONSCIENTIOUS AND GRAPH B IS MORE UNCONVENTIONAL. You are likely feeling pressured to produce at a rate that precludes the accuracy and high standards that are natural for you. Having more of an opportunity to process details and research facts will reduce stress.

13. *Matching Job Settings with Personality Tendencies*

The **ADAPTIVE-DIRECTING** dimension indicates the amount of control and decision-making authority needed at work. In the Job Description, look for the opportunity to:

ADAPTIVE	**DIRECTING**
• Adapt to others' agenda	• Set the agenda
• Cooperate	• Compete
• Move slowly into new areas	• Move quickly to get results
• Be tactful	• Be bold
• Focus on one thing at a time	• See the global perspective
• Complete the current task	• Take on new challenges

The **RESERVED-INTERACTING** dimension indicates the degree of social interaction needed at work. In the Job Description, look for the opportunity to:

RESERVED	**INTERACTING**
• Work alone or one-on-one	• Meet new people
• Be serious	• Be enthusiastic
• Be practical	• Be optimistic
• Not worry about what others think	• Make a good impression
• Be modest	• Be in the limelight
• Work quietly and/or listen	• Be talkative

The **OBJECTIVE-SUPPORTIVE** dimension indicates the amount of harmony and stability needed at work. In the Job Description, look for the opportunity to:

OBJECTIVE	**SUPPORTIVE**
• Use logic over feelings	• Show feelings—favor empathy
• Be tough-minded	• Be warm and compassionate
• Be independent and self-reliant	• Be supportive of others
• Operate in conflict	• Promote harmony
• Be eager	• Be patient
• Be dynamic	• Be even-paced

The **UNCONVENTIONAL-CONSCIENTIOUS** dimension indicates the degree of structure and detail needed at work. In the Job Description, look for the opportunity to:

UNCONVENTIONAL	**CONSCIENTIOUS**
• Be spontaneous and unstructured	• Be organized and structured
• Be flexible and versatile	• Be predictable
• Be unconventional	• Be conventional
• Work with concepts and generalities	• Work with specifics and details
• Rely on instincts	• Conduct research to determine facts
• Take a risk	• Take a cautious approach

MORE ON **AROU** AND **DISC**

OUTGOING-GENERALIST
Control the conversation
Change the environment
Spontaneous
Unstructured
High energy
Fast-paced
Initiating

	D	**I**	
	O	U	
	—	—	
	R	A	
	C	**S**	

TASK-ORIENTED
Cold
Tough-minded
Intense
Results-oriented
Suspicious

PEOPLE-ORIENTED
Warm
Agreeable
Relaxed
Feelings-oriented
Trusting

RESERVED-SPECIALIST
Listen to others
Maintain the environment
Like time to prepare
Structured
Low energy
Slow-paced
Supportive

*(For simplicity of explanation, the following discussion will refer only to the **DISC** terms. By looking in the appropriate **DISC** quadrant, however, you can relate the discussion to the **AROU** terms.)*

As the above chart indicates, **D** and **I** profiles share many characteristics. They both tend to be outgoing, active, and expressive. Typically, their thoughts are directed outward toward projects, people, and challenges. Both **D** and **I** are typically energized by change, variety, and new encounters.

C and **S** profiles tend to be reserved and are more likely to listen, respond, and support, rather than try to control the conversation or activity. They also are much more introspective and more comfortable in their own private world. **C** and **S** personalities are de-energized by having to be "social" in public situations. Their socialization needs are met much better by sharing in a more private setting with a close friend.

31

D and **C** personalities share a focus on tasks and tend to operate from a more cold-and-calculating perspective. They tend to be serious, matter-of-fact, and very results-oriented. They are likely to be analytical and project-oriented and, therefore, are well suited to solving complex problems.

I and **S** personalities share a focus on people. They are motivated to be accepting of others, and they tend to be naturally sensitive to the feelings of other people. Their warm, congenial attitude makes it easy for them to encourage others.

Relating Personality to Career Decisions

Look at the diagram on the previous page and review similarities and differences among the four dimensions of **D**, **I**, **S**, and **C**. Note that **D**s and **C**s share the characteristics of being task-oriented, and I and S personalities tend to be people-oriented.

Those who are people-oriented have a natural desire to interact with others in a helpful way. Given a choice between doing a non-person-related task or directly assisting a person, they would prefer to get involved with the person. The **I** and **S** personalities probably would prefer to work with a group of people.

A task-oriented person can have just as great a love for others as anyone else but would prefer to help by doing something that does not involve people. For instance, a task-oriented person could have a great burden for others and help them by working for years in a lab to develop a new vaccine. And a task-oriented person would invest years in translating the Bible into a new language so an obscure tribe could read the Word of God.

1. Are you more task-oriented or people-oriented? Evaluate statements a and b and select the one that applies.

    a._____ *I am motivated more toward completing tasks.*

Task-oriented people are usually focused on seeing specific results. They like closure and being able to see what they have accomplished. They tend to be focused, intense, serious, suspicious, and tough-minded about business deals. They prefer to work alone so they will not be interrupted in their efforts.

    b._____ *I am motivated more toward the needs of people.*

Those who are more people-oriented are usually warm, accepting, agreeable, relaxed, sensitive to the feelings of others, trusting, open, soft-hearted, less time-sensitive, and less pressed for closure.

2. How does your answer to the previous question compare with your personality strengths? How will it affect your consideration of occupational choices?

_____

_____

_____.

When we look at the way **D**, **I**, **S**, and **C** personalities operate in relation to others, we see them dividing up differently. **S** personalities and **C** personalities are similar in that they tend to be reserved and inwardly focused in their thinking. **D** personalities and I personalities, on the other hand, tend to be more outgoing and externally focused.

Given that piece of information, you can see why **S** and **C** personalities are often involved in research or skilled crafts, and **D** and **I** personalities are more likely to be involved in automobile sales or management training. One group tends to focus on thinking through or doing the task at hand; the other enjoys getting others to think about or do something.

3. Are you more outgoing or reserved?

a._____ _I tend to be outgoing (extroverted) in my thinking and actions._

Outgoing people generally focus on getting others to do something by persuading, directing, exhorting, motivating, encouraging, leading, delegating, and talking. Additionally, outgoing people tend to focus blame for their mistakes in an outward direction (on others).

b._____ _I tend to be reserved (introspective) in my thinking and actions._

Reserved people generally focus on thoughts and activities related to their own performance and personal world rather than others'. They operate by thinking, contemplating, studying, analyzing, moving slowly, using caution, listening, following instructions, and focusing on the task at hand. They like time alone to recharge, and they are likely to focus blame for their mistakes more on themselves than on others.

4. How does your answer to question 3 compare with your personality strengths? How will it affect your consideration of occupations?

_____

_____

_____

_____.

Another way of looking at personality is in terms of being a **generalist** or a **specialist**. The idea of generalists and specialists is in itself a generalization, but we have found it a convenient and fairly accurate way to relate to the types of work people do.

Generalists have a knack for quickly grasping broad principles and applying them in a general way. They tend to operate in a conceptual mode, as opposed to a detailed mode, and their thinking typically operates in a deductive manner. They see the big picture, reach a conclusion, and make intuitive assumptions about the supporting details.

Specialists, on the other hand, tend to focus deeply on a subject in order to fully investigate, validate, and understand the operating details. They will tend to be inductive in their thinking, moving step-by-step through the specifics to arrive at a conclusion.

5. Based on what you know about your personality strengths and weaknesses, consider the following work activities and respond YES or NO in the space provided.

a._____ *Would you be comfortable in occupations that require regular interaction with strangers in social and professional settings?*

b._____ *Are you energized by frequent changes in your work responsibilities and work setting?*

c._____ *Do you find it easy to initiate conversations or make small talk with strangers?*

d._____ *Do you tend to take the lead in committee meetings when things get off course?*

e._____ *Does it energize you to think about taking on a new challenge?*

f._____ *Do you find it easy to understand broad concepts but bothersome to follow detailed explanations?*

g._____ *Does it come naturally for you to make decisions for the group?*

h._____ *Do you enjoy projects on which you work alone?*

i. _____ *Are you self-disciplined about setting schedules and getting tasks done on time?*

j. _____ *Do you make sure that a job is done to high standards whether it's a routine or important task?*

k._____ *Is it important for you to be very well-trained for a task before you assume responsibility for it?*

l._____ *Is it important for you to have time to think through your work very thoroughly before taking action?*

m._____ *Do you seek out the facts before coming to conclusions, rather than rely on your general knowledge?*

n._____ *Do you tend to be patient and cautious in your work to avoid the risk of making a mistake?*

Go back and look at your answers. More than likely, most of your answers for questions **a** through **g** were opposite from your responses on **h** through **n**. Questions **a** through **g** are typically answered YES by those who naturally operate as **generalists**; questions **h** through **n** are typically answered YES by those who naturally operate more as **specialists**.

6. Based on your answers to the questions above, would you say that your tendency is to be

_____**a.** *Clearly a generalist?*

_____**b.** *Primarily a generalist but with specialist characteristics?*

_____**c.** *Clearly a specialist?*

_____**d.** *Primarily a specialist but with generalist characteristics?*

Quite often we see that the problems someone is having at work are related to his or her being a specialist, working in a generalist occupation (and vice versa).

A typical example would be someone who is by nature a scientist or engineer (specialist) getting promoted into a management position (generalist) where he or she has to make a lot of on-the-spot decisions, solve people problems, go to meetings, and act "political" at social events. These activities can be very de-motivating for someone who is a pure specialist.

We should point out that a specialist can be a good manager, but he or she will need to operate differently than a generalist would in the same job. An understanding boss and good role models will be important. It's also important for both specialist and generalist to recognize stress points and delegate responsibility for covering some of them to appropriately matched staff members.

You should use your answers to the questions above to further analyze the type of work you would enjoy. Remember, however, no matter which way your pattern is shaped, your talents are equally important in the workplace and in carrying out the Great Commission.

Rejoice in Your Strengths

Most of us want to feel that our work is contributing to the benefit of others. But did you ever stop to think that we each are equipped to benefit others in different ways? Two people may be motivated equally to serve others; yet, they might approach it quite differently. Consider the following examples.

Jane is a teacher at a community college. She loves her work and especially the opportunity to influence a large number of young people who come into her classes each year. She also serves on two important committees at the college, where she has had an impact on improving the quality of career guidance that students receive. Additionally, in her spare time, Jane serves as the recruiter/coordinator for all nursery workers in her church.

Betty has a totally different personality; yet, she desires to serve others just as much as Jane. Betty originally received her training as an accountant. For 17 years she was a homemaker and prepared income tax returns as a part-time business at home. She faithfully plays the piano for the children's choir at church.

Not long ago Betty reentered the full-time workforce in the accounting department for a local agribusiness corporation. She started slowly but has proved to be an excellent employee. Betty's personality is reserved and she's a good listener.

People find it easy to talk with Betty and, consequently, feel safe in sharing their problems with her. While seeking Betty's counsel for personal problems, two people in the office have come to know the joy of a personal relationship with Jesus Christ. Through Betty's friendship, another lady who had grown cold in her relationship with the Lord was restored and began going to church again.

These examples are typical of how two people serve others with their talents but in totally different ways. Jane was given talents that are more "up-front," and so she's quite visible in the community. Betty carries out her mission quietly and out of the limelight. Yet, it would be a mistake for Betty to compare herself to Jane. Betty has been equipped for a role that is just as important—only different.

We encourage you not to compare yourself to others. It's especially important that those of you who tend to be reserved and task-oriented don't feel guilty or shortchanged if you prefer working alone quietly or one-on-one with close acquaintances.

We never know how God is going to use our efforts in His big picture. It may be that He will use a person like Betty to sow the seeds that will bring us the next Billy Graham. All God asks of us is that we faithfully use what He has given us and that we do it with excellence. He takes care of the results.

FOLLOW THROUGH

In this chapter, as well as Chapters 4, 5, and 6, you will be given "Follow Through" instructions to transfer your results to the *Action Plan Summary* in Chapter 7. When you see these instructions, stop and complete the information transfer before proceeding.

1. Transfer your list of strengths and weaknesses from page P-20 of the Personality I.D. section to the appropriate blanks on page A-2 of the *Action Plan Summary*.

2. Transfer your answers to questions 1, 3, 6 on pages 32 to 35 to the appropriate spaces on page A-2 of the *Action Plan Summary* in Chapter 7.

CHAPTER
4

UNDERSTANDING YOUR SKILLS

In this chapter you'll look closely at your skills and abilities. Don't be surprised if there is a strong relationship between your personality strengths and your strongest abilities. Since personality is tied to motivations, it tends to facilitate activities that come naturally and in which we excel.

The Skills Survey in this chapter is designed to help you identify three types of skills or abilities. First, you will list your **job skills**—the specific skills you have used in previous employment. Just because you've done them doesn't mean they are well suited for your future career.

The second type of skills you'll look at is **transferable skills**. These are general processes that can be transferred to several career fields. For instance, a teacher who is a good communicator could use those skills in a number of corporate and institutional settings.

Transferable skills should be important criteria when choosing a career objective and should be highlighted in your résumé.

Finally, you will look at **self-management skills**. These will contribute to your long-term success on the job because they relate to character and maturity.

Instructions: Turn the page and work through the Skills Survey. As with all the surveys, please follow the instructions carefully.

A guide to identifying your skills and abilities

A product of Life Pathways
The Career Outreach of
Christian Financial Concepts
PO Box 1476
Gainesville, GA 30503
(770) 534-1000

Name _____

Date _____

Skills Survey

The Purpose of This Survey

A skill is an ability to do something. All of us have a number of skills, but we might have a difficult time naming them if we were asked. Knowing what your skills are will be very important to you when you seek employment. When an employer considers you, one question he or she is going to ask is "What are your skills?" Your skills are what you have to contribute to the company. If you have skills that the company needs, you can pass the first hurdle in the job search process.

One way to determine your strongest skills is to categorize them into three groups: Job Skills, Transferable Skills, and Self-Management Skills. This survey will help you determine your skills in each of these groups. Simply follow the directions for each section.

Section One: Job Skills

Job Skills are skills that you've used in previous employment, volunteer work, or hobbies. For example, a farmer needs to know how to plant crops and harvest crops. These skills may have been acquired through experience and/or education.

Some Examples of Job Skills

Cut/Style hair	Sell automobiles
Repair car engines	Manage a work team
Take blood pressure	Calculate employee benefits
Type/File	Counsel drug addicts
Interpret laws	Perform surgery
Edit/Proofread books and articles	Sell life insurance
Write a weekly column	Design aircraft systems
Drive a tractor trailer truck	Fly an airplane
Prepare lesson plans	Grow crops

INSTRUCTIONS: Think of your four strongest job skills and list them in the spaces below. Remember, job skills are very specific and involve activities you now do or have done in the past. These skills may or may not involve your best talents.

1.

2.

3.

4.

Skills Survey

Section Two: Transferable Skills

Transferable Skills are skills that can be used in many different jobs. You may transfer these skills from one job to a completely different job, and the skills will still be effective tools.

INSTRUCTIONS: Rate the following Transferable Skills according to your ability to perform them. Remember, you will not excel in every area. This will simply help you to determine where your greatest skills are.

Check the appropriate block to identify the strength of your abilities.
1 is little or no ability
5 is very high ability

Transferable Skills

High Ability

No Ability

	1	2	3	4	5	
1. Perform athletically	☐	☐	☐	☐	☐	___
2. Perform routine functions	☐	☐	☐	☐	☐	___
3. Perform musically	☐	☐	☐	☐	☐	___
4. Start a business	☐	☐	☐	☐	☐	___
5. Understand complex subjects	☐	☐	☐	☐	☐	___
6. Handle complaints	☐	☐	☐	☐	☐	___
7. Use physical strength	☐	☐	☐	☐	☐	___
8. Count	☐	☐	☐	☐	☐	___
9. Edit	☐	☐	☐	☐	☐	___
10. Sell	☐	☐	☐	☐	☐	___
11. Investigate	☐	☐	☐	☐	☐	___
12. Nurture	☐	☐	☐	☐	☐	___
13. Work with animals	☐	☐	☐	☐	☐	___
14. Work with details	☐	☐	☐	☐	☐	___
15. Present artistic ideas	☐	☐	☐	☐	☐	___
16. Plan	☐	☐	☐	☐	☐	___
17. Analyze	☐	☐	☐	☐	☐	___
18. Entertain people	☐	☐	☐	☐	☐	___
19. Use hands skillfully	☐	☐	☐	☐	☐	___
20. File records	☐	☐	☐	☐	☐	___

After you have evaluated all 120 items, use this space
to identify your top nine transferable skills.

Skills Survey

Transferable Skills

	1	2	3	4	5
21. Visualize	☐	☐	☐	☐	☐
22. Delegate	☐	☐	☐	☐	☐
23. Understand scientific theories	☐	☐	☐	☐	☐
24. Interview/question people	☐	☐	☐	☐	☐
25. Assemble things	☐	☐	☐	☐	☐
26. Calculate/compute	☐	☐	☐	☐	☐
27. Create	☐	☐	☐	☐	☐
28. Influence others	☐	☐	☐	☐	☐
29. Develop new theories	☐	☐	☐	☐	☐
30. Recruit people	☐	☐	☐	☐	☐
31. Handle heavy materials	☐	☐	☐	☐	☐
32. Follow directions	☐	☐	☐	☐	☐
33. Write expressively	☐	☐	☐	☐	☐
34. Coordinate projects	☐	☐	☐	☐	☐
35. Solve abstract problems	☐	☐	☐	☐	☐
36. Mediate problems	☐	☐	☐	☐	☐
37. Operate machines	☐	☐	☐	☐	☐
38. Keep financial records	☐	☐	☐	☐	☐
39. Use imagination	☐	☐	☐	☐	☐
40. Negotiate	☐	☐	☐	☐	☐
41. Research	☐	☐	☐	☐	☐
42. Entertain/host	☐	☐	☐	☐	☐
43. Work with tools	☐	☐	☐	☐	☐
44. Work efficiently	☐	☐	☐	☐	☐
45. Sketch	☐	☐	☐	☐	☐
46. Take calculated risks	☐	☐	☐	☐	☐
47. Work methodically	☐	☐	☐	☐	☐
48. Arrange social functions	☐	☐	☐	☐	☐
49. Paint buildings	☐	☐	☐	☐	☐
50. Take inventory	☐	☐	☐	☐	☐

*After you have evaluated all 120 items, use this space
to identify your top nine transferable skills.*

Skills Survey

Transferable Skills

		1	2	3	4	5	
51.	Invent	☐	☐	☐	☐	☐	___
52.	Run meetings	☐	☐	☐	☐	☐	___
53.	Use curiosity	☐	☐	☐	☐	☐	___
54.	Teach	☐	☐	☐	☐	☐	___
55.	Repair things	☐	☐	☐	☐	☐	___
56.	Provide stability	☐	☐	☐	☐	☐	___
57.	Perform/act	☐	☐	☐	☐	☐	___
58.	Manage/direct others	☐	☐	☐	☐	☐	___
59.	Work alone	☐	☐	☐	☐	☐	___
60.	Motivate people	☐	☐	☐	☐	☐	___
61.	Service equipment	☐	☐	☐	☐	☐	___
62.	Record facts/data	☐	☐	☐	☐	☐	___
63.	Paint (artist)	☐	☐	☐	☐	☐	___
64.	Get results	☐	☐	☐	☐	☐	___
65.	Improve things	☐	☐	☐	☐	☐	___
66.	Use tact	☐	☐	☐	☐	☐	___
67.	Use practical solutions	☐	☐	☐	☐	☐	___
68.	Recall information	☐	☐	☐	☐	☐	___
69.	Sculpt	☐	☐	☐	☐	☐	___
70.	Set up/write procedures	☐	☐	☐	☐	☐	___
71.	Work precisely	☐	☐	☐	☐	☐	___
72.	Counsel people	☐	☐	☐	☐	☐	___
73.	Craft articles for sale	☐	☐	☐	☐	☐	___
74.	Appraise a service/job	☐	☐	☐	☐	☐	___
75.	Perform (artistic)	☐	☐	☐	☐	☐	___
76.	Speak in public	☐	☐	☐	☐	☐	___
77.	Use logic	☐	☐	☐	☐	☐	___
78.	Encourage/exhort	☐	☐	☐	☐	☐	___
79.	Drive/operate vehicles	☐	☐	☐	☐	☐	___
80.	Inspect products	☐	☐	☐	☐	☐	___

*After you have evaluated all 120 items, use this space
to identify your top nine transferable skills.*

Skills Survey

Transferable Skills

		1	2	3	4	5	
81.	Illustrate	☐	☐	☐	☐	☐	___
82.	Initiate new tasks	☐	☐	☐	☐	☐	___
83.	Observe/inspect	☐	☐	☐	☐	☐	___
84.	Provide customer service	☐	☐	☐	☐	☐	___
85.	Build things	☐	☐	☐	☐	☐	___
86.	Purchase products/services	☐	☐	☐	☐	☐	___
87.	Compose/author	☐	☐	☐	☐	☐	___
88.	Display self-confidence	☐	☐	☐	☐	☐	___
89.	Use mathematics	☐	☐	☐	☐	☐	___
90.	Advise	☐	☐	☐	☐	☐	___
91.	Use mechanical skills	☐	☐	☐	☐	☐	___
92.	Organize	☐	☐	☐	☐	☐	___
93.	Express ideas	☐	☐	☐	☐	☐	___
94.	Confront others	☐	☐	☐	☐	☐	___
95.	Locate answers/information	☐	☐	☐	☐	☐	___
96.	Communicate	☐	☐	☐	☐	☐	___
97.	Lift heavy packages	☐	☐	☐	☐	☐	___
98.	Use telephone etiquette	☐	☐	☐	☐	☐	___
99.	Invent new products	☐	☐	☐	☐	☐	___
100.	Respond diplomatically	☐	☐	☐	☐	☐	___
101.	Compare data	☐	☐	☐	☐	☐	___
102.	Care for people	☐	☐	☐	☐	☐	___
103.	Use hand-eye coordination	☐	☐	☐	☐	☐	___
104.	Write clearly	☐	☐	☐	☐	☐	___
105.	Design	☐	☐	☐	☐	☐	___
106.	Lead people	☐	☐	☐	☐	☐	___
107.	Audit records	☐	☐	☐	☐	☐	___
108.	Assist others	☐	☐	☐	☐	☐	___
109.	Produce products	☐	☐	☐	☐	☐	___
110.	Schedule	☐	☐	☐	☐	☐	___

*After you have evaluated all 120 items, use this space
to identify your top nine transferable skills.*

Skills Survey

Transferable Skills

High Ability

No Ability

	1	2	3	4	5	
111. Draw (art)	☐	☐	☐	☐	☐	___
112. Persuade	☐	☐	☐	☐	☐	___
113. Classify ideas/information	☐	☐	☐	☐	☐	___
114. Guide people	☐	☐	☐	☐	☐	___
115. Use complex equipment	☐	☐	☐	☐	☐	___
116. Manage money	☐	☐	☐	☐	☐	___
117. Dance	☐	☐	☐	☐	☐	___
118. Articulate	☐	☐	☐	☐	☐	___
119. Comprehend (intellectual)	☐	☐	☐	☐	☐	___
120. Coach/train others	☐	☐	☐	☐	☐	___

After you have evaluated all 120 items, use this space to identify your top nine transferable skills.

INSTRUCTIONS: Look back over the transferable skills you rated highest, identify your nine strongest, and record them in the spaces below. These most likely will come from those you rated "5" or "4."

1.	4.	7.
2.	5.	8.
3.	6.	9.

Section Three: Self-Management Skills

Self-Management Skills are usually an indication of maturity and character. They encompass every aspect of life, including personality, training, experience, and spiritual commitment. Although Job Skills and Transferable Skills usually decide whether a person can do a job, Self-Management Skills may determine the manner in which the person will do the job.

INSTRUCTIONS: Rate the following Self-Management Skills according to your ability to perform them. Check the appropriate block to identify the strength of your abilities.

Skills Survey

Self-Management Skills

	No Ability	1	2	3	4	High Ability 5

1. Alert
2. Calm
3. Competent
4. Compliant
5. Concerned
6. Continually growing
7. Cooperative
8. Courteous
9. Dedicated
10. Dependable
11. Discreet
12. Eager
13. Educated
14. Efficient
15. Encouraging
16. Exceptional
17. Flexible
18. Friendly
19. Hard worker
20. Helpful
21. Honest
22. Industrious
23. Loyal
24. Mature
25. Motivated
26. Neat
27. Open-minded
28. Organized
29. Perfectionist
30. Persevering

*After you have evaluated all 48 items, use this space
to identify your top six self-management skills.*

Skills Survey

Self-Management Skills

	No Ability				High Ability	
	1	2	3	4	5	
31. Positive attitude	☐	☐	☐	☐	☐	___
32. Prepared	☐	☐	☐	☐	☐	___
33. Punctual	☐	☐	☐	☐	☐	___
34. Reliable	☐	☐	☐	☐	☐	___
35. Resourceful	☐	☐	☐	☐	☐	___
36. Respectful of authority	☐	☐	☐	☐	☐	___
37. Responsible	☐	☐	☐	☐	☐	___
38. Self-confident	☐	☐	☐	☐	☐	___
39. Self-disciplined	☐	☐	☐	☐	☐	___
40. Self-motivated	☐	☐	☐	☐	☐	___
41. Sense of humor	☐	☐	☐	☐	☐	___
42. Sincere	☐	☐	☐	☐	☐	___
43. Tactful	☐	☐	☐	☐	☐	___
44. Trained	☐	☐	☐	☐	☐	___
45. Trustworthy	☐	☐	☐	☐	☐	___
46. Willing (to learn)	☐	☐	☐	☐	☐	___
47. Willing (to change)	☐	☐	☐	☐	☐	___
48. Well-informed	☐	☐	☐	☐	☐	___

INSTRUCTIONS: Review the skills you rated as strong, determine your six strongest Self-Management Skills, and list them below. These skills will be extremely important to a potential employer. Be sure you mention these in interviews and correspondence with such employers.

1.	3.	5.
2.	4.	6.

Transfer the skills you have selected on page S-2, page S-7, and those above to the appropriate blanks for skills in the Action Plan Summary, pages A-2 and A-3.

FOLLOW THROUGH

Be sure you have transferred the results of your **Skills Survey** to the skills section on pages A-2 and A-3 of the *Action Plan Summary* in Chapter 7.

Before leaving this chapter, stop for a moment to review your transferable and self-management skills.

In general, do the two groups relate and, if so, how?

_____

_____

_____ .

How do they compare to your personality strengths? Identify any relationships you see at this point. (See page P-20, Personality I.D.)

_____

_____

_____ .

Look back at the self-management skills you rated low and identify any you may need to work on to improve your effectiveness. (See pages S-8 and S-9, Skills Survey.)

1._____

2._____

3._____

4._____

Skills Are Critical to Employment

Your skills and abilities are the basis for your employment, so it's critical for you to know what they are. They should be highlighted in your résumé and in any conversation with a potential employer.

Remember, employers hire for one reason: They are looking for someone who can fill a particular need in their organization and, thereby, help them to make more money or better fulfill their mission. They don't hire someone just because that person is nice. They want someone who can fulfill a specific role.

When you know your skills and you know they match the job you are considering, you will have confidence in your ability to do the job well. Your excitement and confidence will be evident during an interview and may be the edge you need to get the job that fits you.

Good Stewardship of Your Skills and Abilities

The foundation for your talents is your endowment from God. He created you to do certain processes and functions well because He has called you to fulfill a special role in His kingdom on earth.

The Bible teaches us to develop and improve what we've been given. The parable of the talents in Matthew 25 relates this stewardship principle: We are to invest our talents and not bury them.

To invest your skills and abilities means to develop them and use them. Part of your life's plan should be a commitment to the continuing development of your God-given talents.

Spiritually and practically, there are rewards for being a good steward of your talents; so we challenge you to examine how you might make better use of yours.

CHAPTER
5

UNDERSTANDING YOUR WORK PRIORITIES

This chapter will focus on your work priorities and life values. Don't be concerned if there seems to be some overlap with other surveys. Although they may look similar, each survey is designed to give you a slightly different view of your pattern. The overlap within the four parts of your pattern (personality, skills, work priorities, vocational interests) will help confirm your strengths and interests.

As you work through this next evaluation, you will be asked to prioritize what is important to you. The more realistic you can be, the better your results will be. It may be helpful to pause from time to time and ask yourself: Why is this important to me? Is it really important to me, or is my interest centered on the importance it holds for others, such as parents, spouse, friends, and mentors?

We raise this question because we see so many people who have chosen occupations to please someone else, only to have a work life of misery and regrets. Motive is of utmost importance in every choice we make. If your motive for favoring one field over another is because that's the way God made you, you can be sure that your innate desires of the heart will be good signposts in your search for career direction.

Turn the page and begin with Section 1 of the Work Priorities Evaluation on page W-2. Remember to follow the instructions.

Life Pathways

A guide to identifying and understanding your career choices

A product of Life Pathways
The Career Outreach of
Christian Financial Concepts
PO Box 1476
Gainesville, GA 30503
(770) 534-1000

Name _____

Date _____

Work Priorities Evaluation

INTRODUCTION

This survey requires you to evaluate what is really important to you. It will help you to discover the underlying values that bring meaning and purpose to your work. Your answers should express the strongest desires of your heart. The more you are able to satisfy these priorities in your work environment, the more satisfied you will be in your work.

Respond below based on what is important to you—not to your friends or to your family, but to you, in your work and in your life.

INSTRUCTIONS: Rate each of the following statements from 1 to 5, with 1 meaning "NOT important," and 5 meaning "MOST important."

I. *You probably have many of the abilities listed below. Evaluate how important it is for you to use these abilities in order to enjoy your work.*

MOST important

NOT important

	1	2	3	4	5
1. Speak, convince, sell, teach—communicate verbally	☐	☐	☐	☐	☐
2. Compose, write, edit—communicate in writing	☐	☐	☐	☐	☐
3. Play sports or dance—athletics	☐	☐	☐	☐	☐
4. Investigate, analyze facts and data—research	☐	☐	☐	☐	☐
5. Develop new ideas, author, invent, develop—create	☐	☐	☐	☐	☐
6. Sing, act, entertain—perform	☐	☐	☐	☐	☐
7. Direct, coordinate, supervise—lead or manage	☐	☐	☐	☐	☐
8. Draw, paint, design—art	☐	☐	☐	☐	☐
9. Construct, build, sew, weave—crafts	☐	☐	☐	☐	☐
10. Type, file, use computer—clerical	☐	☐	☐	☐	☐
11. Use technical knowledge with equipment/software—technical	☐	☐	☐	☐	☐
12. Operate or repair machines and equipment—mechanical	☐	☐	☐	☐	☐
13. Translate, write, interpret—use foreign language skills	☐	☐	☐	☐	☐
14. Other _____	☐	☐	☐	☐	☐

Review your choices and indicate your top four choices in the spaces provided.

Work Priorities Evaluation

II. *We all have preferred working environments. Rate the following conditions and situations for their importance to your work satisfaction.*

NOT important   MOST important

	1	2	3	4	5	
1. Stability	☐	☐	☐	☐	☐	___
2. Challenge, intellectual	☐	☐	☐	☐	☐	___
3. Challenge, physical	☐	☐	☐	☐	☐	___
4. Travel	☐	☐	☐	☐	☐	___
5. Outdoors	☐	☐	☐	☐	☐	___
6. Flexibility	☐	☐	☐	☐	☐	___
7. Harmony	☐	☐	☐	☐	☐	___
8. Variety	☐	☐	☐	☐	☐	___
9. Security	☐	☐	☐	☐	☐	___
10. Adventure/Risk	☐	☐	☐	☐	☐	___
11. Cleanliness	☐	☐	☐	☐	☐	___
12. Organization	☐	☐	☐	☐	☐	___
13. Indoors	☐	☐	☐	☐	☐	___
14. International	☐	☐	☐	☐	☐	___
15. Other _____	☐	☐	☐	☐	☐	___

Review your choices and indicate your top four choices in the spaces provided.

III. *Work Activities—What are the tools, means, or processes you want to use in your work?*

	1	2	3	4	5	
1. Work with machines or equipment	☐	☐	☐	☐	☐	___
2. Work with numbers or math	☐	☐	☐	☐	☐	___
3. Work with ideas, concepts, or principles	☐	☐	☐	☐	☐	___
4. Work with my hands	☐	☐	☐	☐	☐	___
5. Work with people: adults	☐	☐	☐	☐	☐	___
6. Work with people: children	☐	☐	☐	☐	☐	___
7. Work with arts/crafts	☐	☐	☐	☐	☐	___
8. Work with music	☐	☐	☐	☐	☐	___
9. Work with animals	☐	☐	☐	☐	☐	___
10. Other _____	☐	☐	☐	☐	☐	___

Review your choices and indicate your top four choices in the spaces provided.

Work Priorities Evaluation

NOT important

MOST important

NOT important

IV. *What is the purpose of your life? What outcomes do you value most?*

	1	2	3	4	5	
1. Becoming financially well-off	☐	☐	☐	☐	☐	___
2. Being honest in all I do, having integrity	☐	☐	☐	☐	☐	___
3. Gaining recognition and prestige	☐	☐	☐	☐	☐	___
4. Serving God through everything I do	☐	☐	☐	☐	☐	___
5. Providing and caring for my family	☐	☐	☐	☐	☐	___
6. Achieving results that demonstrate my abilities	☐	☐	☐	☐	☐	___
7. Having a nice home, car, clothes, and traveling	☐	☐	☐	☐	☐	___
8. Helping others	☐	☐	☐	☐	☐	___
9. Continuing to grow and develop	☐	☐	☐	☐	☐	___
10. Other _____	☐	☐	☐	☐	☐	___

Review your choices and indicate your top four choices (1, 2, 3, 4) in the spaces provided.

V. *Work Priorities Summary*

Write your top four priorities from Sections I through IV.

Section A — Abilities

1. _____
2. _____
3. _____
4. _____

Section C — Work Activities

1. _____
2. _____
3. _____
4. _____

Section B — Environment

1. _____
2. _____
3. _____
4. _____

Section D — Purpose

1. _____
2. _____
3. _____
4. _____

Transfer your Work Priorities Summary from V above to the Work Priorities section of the Action Plan Summary, page A–3.

FOLLOW THROUGH

Be sure you have transferred the results of your **Work Priorities Summary** section to page A-3 of the *Action Plan Summary* in Chapter 7.

Analyze Your Work Priorities

This critical step will assist you in gaining the greatest applications from the Work Priorities Evaluation for you, your developing career, and your life's direction.

1. Pause for a moment and analyze Section V of your Work Priorities Summary.

a. Look at the relationship of the *Abilities,* Section I (specific skills you desire to use at work) and the *Work Activities,* Section III (the broader processes you want to be involved in at work) that are important to you. In what ways are they similar?

_____

_____

_____.

In what ways are they different?

_____

_____.

How do you account for the differences, if any?

_____

_____.

b. Do your choices for a work environment (Section II) *complement* your choices for Sections I and III? How?

_____

_____

_____.

c. When you look at your top four priorities in Section IV, *Your Life Purpose*, do they represent the way you actually have been living, or are they the way you would like to live? (See Romans 7:19, 23–25.) **Note:** It may help to review the graphic below before answering this question.

_____

_____

_____.

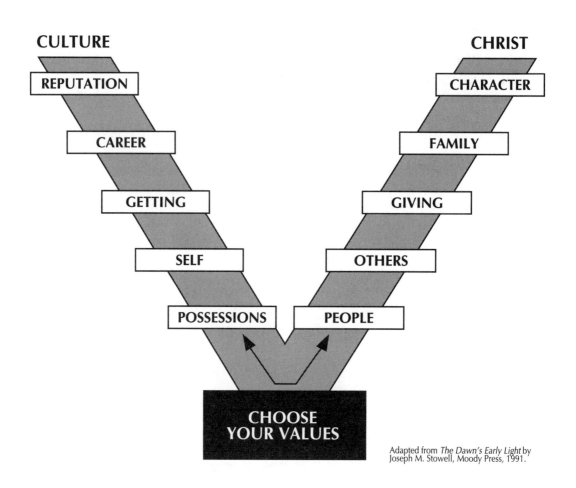

CULTURE

REPUTATION

CAREER

GETTING

SELF

POSSESSIONS

CHRIST

CHARACTER

FAMILY

GIVING

OTHERS

PEOPLE

CHOOSE YOUR VALUES

Adapted from *The Dawn's Early Light* by Joseph M. Stowell, Moody Press, 1991.

d. If your "walk" has not matched your "talk," what will you do differently in the future to bring your life in line with your priorities in order to fulfill your life purpose?

_____

_____

_____.

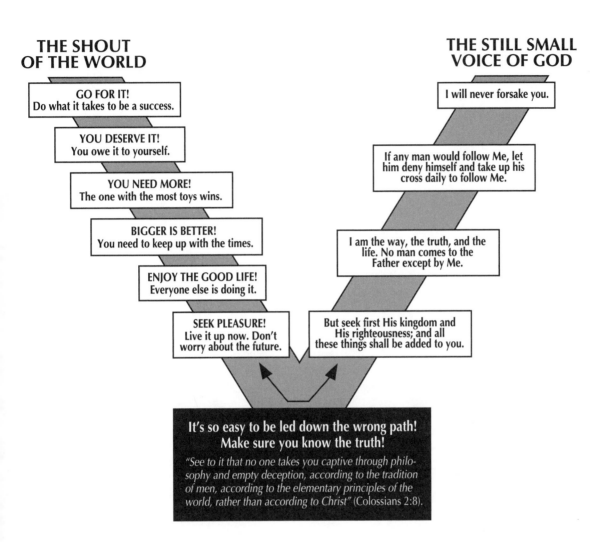

THE SHOUT OF THE WORLD

GO FOR IT!
Do what it takes to be a success.

YOU DESERVE IT!
You owe it to yourself.

YOU NEED MORE!
The one with the most toys wins.

BIGGER IS BETTER!
You need to keep up with the times.

ENJOY THE GOOD LIFE!
Everyone else is doing it.

SEEK PLEASURE!
Live it up now. Don't worry about the future.

THE STILL SMALL VOICE OF GOD

I will never forsake you.

If any man would follow Me, let him deny himself and take up his cross daily to follow Me.

I am the way, the truth, and the life. No man comes to the Father except by Me.

But seek first His kingdom and His righteousness; and all these things shall be added to you.

It's so easy to be led down the wrong path! Make sure you know the truth!

"See to it that no one takes you captive through philosophy and empty deception, according to the tradition of men, according to the elementary principles of the world, rather than according to Christ" (Colossians 2:8).

e. Study the diagram above and analyze which road you are on. Record below your reflections on specific attitudes and priorities you believe need to be altered in order to become a more effective servant for the Lord Jesus Christ (2 Corinthians 10:5).

_____

_____

_____

_____

_____.

"'For I know the plans I have for you,' declares the Lord, 'plans for welfare and not for calamity to give you a future and a hope. Then you will call upon Me and come and pray to Me, and I will listen to you. And you will seek Me and find Me, when you search for Me with all your heart. And I will be found by you,' declares the Lord" (Jeremiah 29:11–14).

CHAPTER
6

UNDERSTANDING YOUR VOCATIONAL INTERESTS

B y now you are well aware that we each have different talents and motivations for work. In this chapter you'll learn more about your motivations by working through the *Vocational Interests Survey*.

It's very important to consider the types of occupations that interest you, because those are usually the ones that hold the highest potential for career success. In fact, there is a good rule of thumb: **The most basic career guidance you can get is to do something you like.**

Motivation Is the Key!

Did you ever notice how easy it is to research, study, and spend time on your hobbies? Effort comes easily because you are motivated toward them. You get involved in hobbies because something about them tweaks your interests. Once you are hooked, your efforts don't seem like work. Consider the following examples.

• Those who like to cook memorize complex recipes, experiment with new dishes, and stand on their feet for hours.

• Sports fans become experts on their favorite teams by memorizing statistics (such as batting averages, shooting percentages, yards per carry, won-lost records) and think little of braving any kind of weather or inconvenience to attend sporting events.

• Coin, stamp, antique, and baseball card collectors become experts by learning history, data, and prices of rare items.

• Woodworkers spend hours meticulously measuring, cutting, sanding, and finishing a new piece of furniture or refinishing an old one.

These seemingly tedious tasks are easy and are enjoyable to people who are motivated to master them. Likewise, work that interests you will be fun, even when it involves tasks that, under other circumstances, would be difficult or boring.

If you are in an occupation that matches your talents, values, and interests, you will look forward to going to work every day.

In this chapter, you will examine seven groups of occupations. As you would expect, these groups are fairly broad in order to cover the many jobs that exist. However, the occupations within each group have many similarities in the nature of the work involved.

By clustering occupations into these seven groups, we've made it easy for you to evaluate various occupations in a general way. Using a sports analogy, these groups will help you to gain quickly an idea of what sport you'd like to play.

Later, you will look deeper at your interests by identifying some possible occupations from a more extensive list. (This would be like deciding which team position would fit your talents.)

Eventually, your research will lead you to potential employers (teams) that might need people like you to complete their lineup.

The occupational groups are explained in the *Vocational Interest Survey*. Each group contains occupations that are similar in nature and are characterized by a one-word title that identifies the general work activity for the group. An understanding of these groups will give you a good framework for evaluating your career interests.

Now complete the *Vocational Interest Survey*.

Vocational **I**nterest **S**urvey

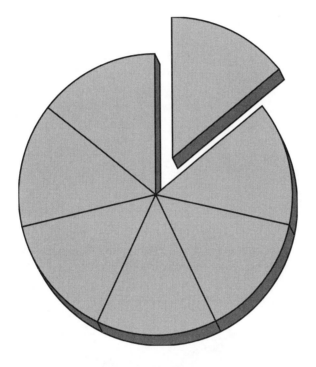

A guide to finding the
career that fits you

A product of Life Pathways
The Career Outreach of
Christian Financial Concepts
PO Box 1476
Gainesville, GA 30503
(770) 534-1000

Name _____

Date _____

DISCOVER YOUR VOCATIONAL INTEREST

We all have unique ideas about the types of work we would consider enjoyable. The purpose of this section is to help you clarify your vocational interests.

In order to help you analyze your interests, this section covers seven occupational groups. These occupational groups are composed of types of work that are similar in nature. Most people typically tend to prefer the type of occupations encompassed by one, two, and sometimes three of these groups.

There is nothing rigid about the seven groups or the occupations in them. They are primarily to give you a framework for thinking about occupations. The next seven pages will cover these groups. As you review each group, try to identify why one may appeal to you more than another and why some may not appeal to you at all. Consider these occupational groups in a very broad sense, based on whether the general types of work appeal to you. This will help you to identify your true vocational interests.

INSTRUCTIONS

Quickly review the seven occupational groups covered on the next seven pages. (You will have the opportunity to look at the occupations in detail later.) **Record your impression of each group in the space provided on each page to show whether your general interest in the group of occupations is "Low," "Average," or "High."**

ADVENTURING

ACTIVITIES SUCH AS PROTECTING, ENFORCING, RISKING

This group has a strong desire to be involved in adventurous, physically challenging, or competitive activities. People who enjoy working in this group of jobs are typically very confident, need excitement, and are not bothered by risks that would intimidate the average person.

People who enjoy occupations in this group typically like to:

* Have physical challenge and adventure at work.
* Perform physical feats as part of work.
* Work where there is occasionally a harsh environment.
* Have work that involves risk and danger.
* Protect the property and lives of others.
* Be involved in rigorous physical training activities.
* Perform duties under emergency situations.

Typical occupations:

Forest fire fighter
Detective
Emergency medical tech
Police officer
Hunting/fishing guide
Stunt artist
Rodeo performer
Acrobat
Equestrian

Military officer
Athletic coach
Professional athlete
Fitness instructor
Test pilot
Umpire
Army ranger/special forces
PE teacher
Flight instructor

MY INTEREST IN THIS GROUP OF OCCUPATIONS IS

_____LOW   _____AVERAGE   _____HIGH

INVESTIGATING

ACTIVITIES SUCH AS ANALYZING, RESEARCHING, STUDYING

People employed in this group of occupations usually enjoy working with scientific theories, mathematical formulas, statistics, and technical applications. This group is more likely than any of the others to pursue knowledge for the sake of knowledge and, therefore, they often gain advanced degrees.

This group of jobs is typically attractive to people who:

* Carry out scientific or medical research.
* Discover new applications for technology.
* Analyze data for research and development.
* Use intellect to learn and synthesize new information into theories.
* Pursue knowledge through advanced degrees.
* Work with technical information and data.
* Use mathematical formulas to solve problems.

Typical occupations:

Environmental scientist
Nurse anesthetist
Physician
Math/science teacher
Systems analyst
Industrial psychologist
Dentist
Computational chemist

Medical technician
Photo-optics technician
Laser technician
Mechanical drafter
Electronic data manager
Dental hygienist
Film laboratory technician
Operating room technician

MY INTEREST IN THIS GROUP OF OCCUPATIONS IS

_____LOW   _____AVERAGE   _____HIGH

CREATING

ARTISTIC ACTIVITIES SUCH AS PAINTING, COMPOSING, AUTHORING

Creative expression is the focus of this occupational group. This creativity can be evidenced through literature, art, music, drama, designing, and similar aesthetic fields of work. People employed in these fields, by their nature, tend to be somewhat unconventional in their approach to life.

Those who enjoy occupations in this group typically like to:

* Draw or design using graphics or art.
* Write a creative work.
* Decorate using color, fashions, or furniture.
* Play a musical instrument or sing at a performance.
* Pursue aesthetic activities such as art, music, and drama.
* Communicate ideas or feelings through fine arts.
* Work with creative ideas.

Typical occupations:

Artist	Author/writer
Musician	Radio/television journalist
Chef	Interior designer
Graphic artist	Music teacher
Photographer	Advertising editor
Video technician	Drama teacher
Choreographer	Commercial artist
Vocalist	Medical illustrator
Painter	Music director
Makeup artist	Cartoon designer

<u>**MY INTEREST IN THIS GROUP OF OCCUPATIONS IS**</u>

_____LOW   _____AVERAGE   _____HIGH

HELPING

ACTIVITIES SUCH AS CARING, GUIDING, TEACHING, NURTURING

The helping group includes work that is oriented toward assisting others to improve their situation. Typical activities include attending to the physical, emotional, or intellectual development or improvement of others. Successful workers in this field are marked by patience, compassion for others, strong listening skills, and a strong desire to help others.

People involved in these occupations usually like to:

* Contribute to the welfare of others.
* Provide assistance to others.
* Help others achieve their potential.
* Coach, train, or influence others.
* Work with people more than things or data.
* Work as a teacher, counselor, social worker, or religious leader.
* Help people solve problems.

Typical occupations:

Physical therapy aide
Homemaker
Cosmetologist/barber
Nurse/midwife
Home economist
Flight attendant
Customer service manager
Recreation leader
Nurse practitioner
Waiter/waitress

Elementary school teacher
Nurse
Counselor/social worker
Family therapist
Guidance counselor
Occupational therapist
Student affairs director
Children's librarian
Dental assistant
Pastor/clergy

MY INTEREST IN THIS GROUP OF OCCUPATIONS IS

_____LOW _____AVERAGE _____HIGH

INFLUENCING

ACTIVITIES SUCH AS PROMOTING, SELLING, MANAGING, PROFITING

This group includes occupations in which work activities focus on influencing others. People who like these types of occupations are generally confident in their abilities to succeed, relish challenge or competition, and have strong communicative and leadership skills.

Those who are successful in these occupations usually like to:

* Lead/manage to accomplish goals.
* Influence others through communicative skills.
* Sell a product or service.
* Have broad responsibility rather than do detail work.
* Pursue activities such as developing, selling, and promoting.
* Pioneer a new product, service, or company.
* Be responsible for the success of an organization.

Typical occupations:

Purchasing agent
Travel agent
Real estate agent
Store manager
Manufacturer's representative
Public relations director
Merchandise manager
Golf club manager
Catering manager

Financial planner
Human resources manager
Attorney (most fields)
Business manager
Corporate trainer
Company president
Labor relations specialist
Hospital administrator
Lobbyist

MY INTEREST IN THIS GROUP OF OCCUPATIONS IS

_____LOW _____AVERAGE _____HIGH

ORGANIZING

ACTIVITIES SUCH AS SCHEDULING, ORDERING, CHECKING

This group of jobs involves activities that make sure the details of the work environment are kept accurate and in good order. People who are successful in these occupations typically are methodical, neat, and structured in their approach.

People in the organizing occupations typically like to:

* Maintain and process information and data.
* Perform clerical functions.
* Follow an established pattern at work.
* Work with information, data, or things more than people.
* Follow procedures rather than lead the group.
* Perform activities such as accounting or administrative services.
* Balance a financial statement or calculate a loan payment.

Typical occupations:

Bank supervisor	Public administrator
Bookkeeper	Auditor/IRS agent
Legal assistant	Insurance underwriter
Dental assistant	Budget analyst
Pharmacy technician	Accountant
Office manager	Business programmer
Mortgage loan clerk	Accounting clerks supervisor
Claims examiner	Television schedule coordinator
Reservations agent	Title examiner

<u>**MY INTEREST IN THIS GROUP OF OCCUPATIONS IS**</u>

_____LOW   _____AVERAGE   _____HIGH

MAKING

ACTIVITIES SUCH AS ASSEMBLING, REPAIRING, GROWING, OPERATING

This group is often rugged and physically strong. They generally prefer achieving practical, tangible, or visible results rather than theoretical or intellectual pursuits. Prefer practical activities that are hands-on, in which the results of work can be seen immediately.

This group of jobs is usually preferred by people who like to:

* Work outdoors in agricultural or mechanical jobs.
* Use hand tools or machines to create or build.
* Drive/operate machinery.
* Perform jobs requiring mechanical or technical skills.
* Work with things more than people or data.
* Be involved in growing crops and/or livestock.
* Repair or build things with their hands.

Typical occupations:

Truck driver	Agribusiness manager
Carpenter	Corporate pilot
Aircraft mechanic	Agriculture teacher
Dental lab technician	Forester
Electrician	Landscape architect
Plumber	Farmer
Tool/die maker	Mail carrier
Appliance repair person	Veterinarian, large animal
Bricklayer	Building contractor
Package technician	Construction inspector

<u>MY INTEREST IN THIS GROUP OF OCCUPATIONS IS</u>		
_____LOW	_____AVERAGE	_____HIGH

WHICH OCCUPATIONAL GROUPS INTEREST YOU MOST?

You have just reviewed seven occupational groups. Most people find they have a strong interest in one, two, and occasionally three of these groups. At this point it would be helpful to evaluate and rank the groups from your highest interests to the lowest. **Look back at your evaluation of each at the bottom of the page, consider the strength of your interest in each, and then list your preferences below.**

LIST YOUR THREE MOST PREFERRED OCCUPATIONAL GROUPS BELOW.

(It's not a problem if they are equally desirable, since you will be looking at them again later.)

1. _____ 2. _____ 3. _____

LIST THE REMAINING PRIORITIES IN ORDER OF PREFERENCE.

4. _____ 6. _____

5. _____ 7. _____

Turn to the next page to further evaluate your interests.

REFINE YOUR INTERESTS

To refine your career interests further, identify four occupations in each of your top three groups listed on the previous page.

DIRECTIONS

Look up your three preferred occupational groups in the pages that follow. Select up to four occupations from each group that interest you enough to warrant further investigation and list them below. Feel free to include other occupations (not included in the lists) that you know about and would like to consider.

OCCUPATIONAL INTEREST GROUP I _____

    1. _____

    2. _____

    3. _____

    4. _____

OCCUPATIONAL INTEREST GROUP II _____

    1. _____

    2. _____

    3. _____

    4. _____

OCCUPATIONAL INTEREST GROUP III _____

    1. _____

    2. _____

    3. _____

    4. _____

FOLLOW THROUGH

Before leaving this chapter, transfer your results to the **Vocational Interests** section on page A-4 of the *Action Plan Summary* in Chapter 7.

EXPANDED LIST OF OCCUPATIONS

The following pages provide an expanded list of occupations. They are organized according to the seven occupational groups used earlier in this section. They also are grouped into subgroups for easier reference.

For detailed information on most of these occupations, refer to the Occupational Outlook Handbook (OOH). This Department of Labor publication provides information on more than 1,200 occupations. It covers the nature of the work involved, working conditions, employment statistics, employment outlook, training and qualifications for advancement, related occupations, and sources of additional information. The OOH is usually available in libraries and career centers and can be accessed on the Internet site (http:// stats.bls.gov/ocohome.htm). Another good source for occupation information is O*NET, the Occupational Information Network. Check with your library or career center for this online database.

ADVENTURING
ACTIVITIES SUCH AS PROTECTING, ENFORCING, RISKING

The distinguishing characteristic of this group is a strong desire to be involved in adventurous, physically challenging, or competitive activities. People who enjoy work activities associated with this group of jobs are typically very confident and are not intimidated by danger or risks. They seem to need this type of excitement to stay motivated in their work.

SAFETY/LAW ENFORCEMENT
- Conservation officer
- Criminal investigator
- Deputy sheriff
- Fire marshal
- Fish and game warden
- Harbormaster
- Police officer
- Special agent
- State highway patrol

SECURITY SERVICES
- Airline security officer
- Armed services, enlisted
- Armored car driver
- Bailiff
- Bodyguard
- Corrections officer/guard/jailer
- Dispatcher
- Fire inspector
- Firefighter
- Military officer
- Private investigator
- S.W.A.T. team
- Security guard
- Ski patroller

AIR/WATER VEHICLE OPERATION
- Airline pilot
- Crop duster pilot
- Fishing vessel captain
- Flight instructor
- Foreign mission pilot
- Helicopter pilot
- Tugboat captain

SPORTS
- Coach
- Fitness instructor
- Hunting and fishing guide
- Mountain climber
- Physical education teacher
- Professional athlete
- Professional scout
- Race car driver
- Ski instructor
- Umpire

PHYSICAL FEATS
- Acrobat
- Equestrian
- Juggler
- Rodeo performer
- Stunt performer

INVESTIGATING
ACTIVITIES SUCH AS ANALYZING, RESEARCHING, STUDYING

People employed in this group of occupations usually enjoy working with scientific theories, mathematical formulas, statistics, and technical applications. Generally, they are happy to work alone and they enjoy research and related activities, such as analysis of data and facts. This group is more likely than any of the others to pursue knowledge for the sake of knowledge and, therefore, they often gain advanced degrees. You might find them teaching or conducting research.

PHYSICAL SCIENCES
- Archaeologist
- Chemist
- Computational chemist
- Geographer
- Geologist
- Hydrologist
- Mathematician
- Metallurgist
- Meteorologist
- Physicist/astronomer
- Seismologist

LIFE SCIENCES
- Animal breeder
- Biologist
- Biomedical engineer
- Botanist
- Dairy scientist
- Ecologist
- Food scientist
- Geneticist
- Pathologist
- Poultry scientist

MEDICAL SCIENCES
- Cardiopulmonary technologist
- Chiropractor
- Dentist
- Medical researcher
- Medical technician
- Operating room technician
- Optometrist
- Optometry assistant
- Orthodontist
- Physician
- Physician assistant
- Podiatrist
- Psychiatrist
- Radiological technician
- Speech pathologist/audiologist
- Veterinarian

LABORATORY TECHNOLOGY
- Chemist
- Embalmer
- Film laboratory technician
- Histologist
- Medical lab technician
- Pharmacist
- Pharmacy technician
- Polygraph examiner
- Toxicologist

ENGINEERING
- Acoustical engineer
- Aerospace engineer
- Agricultural scientist
- Airport engineer
- Architect
- Civil engineer
- Computer specialist
- Electrical engineer
- Electronics engineer
- Environmental scientist
- Landscape architect
- Laser technician
- Nuclear decontamination specialist
- Systems analyst
- Wireless specialist

SOCIAL RESEARCH
- Anthropologist
- Applied psychologist
- Criminologist
- Economist
- Historian
- Occupational analyst
- Personnel recruiter
- Political scientist
- Sociologist
- Urban planner

CREATING
ARTISTIC ACTIVITIES SUCH AS PAINTING, COMPOSING, AUTHORING

This group of occupations focuses on creative expression. This can be evidenced through literature, journalism, art, music, drama, designing, and similar aesthetic fields of work. People employed in these fields, by their nature, tend to be somewhat unconventional in their approach to life.

LITERARY ARTS
- Author/writer
- Biographer
- Columnist
- Critic
- Electronic publishing specialist
- Film editor
- Motion picture producer
- Publications editor

VISUAL ARTS
- Arts administrator
- Audiovisual production specialist
- Cartoonist
- Commercial artist
- Costume designer
- Fashion designer
- Florist
- Graphic artist/designer
- Industrial designer
- Interior decorator/designer
- Medical illustrator
- Photographer/camera operator
- Sculptor

PERFORMING ARTS: DRAMA
- Actor/producer/director
- Comedian
- Drama teacher
- Fine arts specialist
- Radio/TV broadcaster

PERFORMING ARTS: MUSIC
- Composer
- Music arranger
- Music director/conductor
- Music teacher
- Musician/instrumentalist
- Vocalist

PERFORMING ARTS: DANCE
- Ballet dancer
- Choreographer
- Dance instructor
- Dance studio manager

CRAFT ARTS
- Advertising specialist
- Airbrush artist
- Jeweler
- Lithographic photographer
- Painter
- Picture framer
- Sign maker
- Taxidermist

ELEMENTAL ARTS
- Amusement park announcer
- Diver impersonator
- Weight guesser

MODELING
- Extra
- Garment model
- Modeling instructor
- Photographer's model
- Stand-in

COMMUNICATIONS
- Communicator
- Editor, books, and publications
- Interpreter for the deaf
- Journalist
- Newspaper reporter/correspondent
- Radio/TV news reporter
- Translator/interpreter
- Writer/editor

HELPING
ACTIVITIES SUCH AS CARING, GUIDING, TEACHING, NURTURING

The helping group includes work that is oriented toward assisting others to improve their situations. Typical activities include attending to the physical, emotional, or intellectual development or improvements of others. Successful workers in this field are marked by patience, compassion for others, strong listening skills, and a strong desire to help others.

HOSPITALITY SERVICES
- Flight attendant
- Funeral attendant
- Maitre d'/hostess
- Recreation leader
- Restaurant manager
- Waiter/waitress
- YMCA/YWCA directors

BARBER/BEAUTY SERVICES
- Barber
- Cosmetologist
- Hair stylist
- Manicurist

PASSENGER SERVICES
- Bus driver
- Cab supervisor
- Chauffeur
- Driving instructor
- Taxi driver

CUSTOMER SERVICES
- Customer service representative
- Fast food worker
- Furniture deliverer
- Newspaper carrier
- Parking lot attendant
- Sales associate

ATTENDANT SERVICES
- Bellhop/baggage claim attendant
- Caddie
- Cafeteria worker
- Caterer
- Food service manager
- Masseur/masseuse
- Usher/ticket taker

SOCIAL SERVICES
- Caseworker
- Chemical dependency counselor
- Counselor/psychologist
- Director of placement
- Guidance counselor
- Minister
- Religious leader
- Social worker

NURSING, THERAPY/SPECIALIZED TEACHING SERVICES
- Athletic trainer
- Dental hygienist
- Home health aide
- LPN
- Mental health technician
- Nurse practitioner
- Nurse's aide
- Nursing administrator
- Occupational therapist
- Paramedic
- Patient educator/representative
- Physical therapist
- Physician's assistant
- Radiologic technologist
- Registered nurse
- Respiratory therapist
- Respiratory therapist technician
- Special education teacher

CHILD/ADULT CARE
- Child care worker
- Dental assistant
- Emergency medical technician
- Home health aide
- Medical assistant

EDUCATIONAL/LIBRARY SCIENCES
- Adult education teacher
- Art teacher
- College professor
- Cooperative extension manager
- Educational administrator
- Elementary education teacher
- Home economics teacher
- Homemaker
- K – 12 teacher
- Librarian
- Mathematics teacher
- Science teacher
- Social science teacher
- Speech education teacher
- Teacher's aide

INFLUENCING
ACTIVITIES SUCH AS PROMOTING, SELLING, MANAGING, PROFITING

This group includes occupations in which work activities focus on influencing others. This could be through managing, speaking, directing, or related leadership positions, which include a responsibility to bring about results. People who like these types of occupations are generally confident in their abilities to succeed and relish challenges or competition. Strong communicative and leadership skills generally are required in these occupations.

SALES TECHNOLOGY
- Buyer
- Engineering/technical sales agent
- Estate planner
- Financial planner
- Hospitality services sales agent
- Insurance broker
- Life insurance agent
- Pharmaceutical representative
- Sales representative

GENERAL SALES
- Church furniture/supplies salesperson
- Manufacturing representative
- Real estate agent
- Real estate broker
- Retail salesperson
- Telephone sales associate
- Travel agent

LAW
- Abstractor
- Corporate lawyer
- Criminal lawyer
- District attorney
- Intellectual property lawyer
- Judge
- Legal assistant
- Paralegal
- Patent agent

BUSINESS ADMINISTRATION
- Business education manager
- CEO/president
- Corporate personnel trainer
- Dietician
- Hardware store manager
- Health services administrator
- Human resources manager/executive
- Labor relations specialist
- Manufacturing operations manager
- Merchandise manager
- Outplacement consultant
- Personnel director
- Personnel manager
- Research and development manager
- Retail store manager
- Training manager

SERVICES ADMINISTRATION
- Academic dean
- Alcohol/drug abuse center administrator
- Athletic director
- College/university registrar
- Correctional facility superintendent
- Financial aid director
- Hospital administrator
- Medical records administrator
- Member service director
- Nursing home administrator
- Public administrator
- Recreation supervisor
- School administrator
- School superintendent
- Traffic safety director

PROMOTION
- Advertising executive
- Bank marketer
- Chamber of commerce executive
- Fund-raising director
- Marketing director
- Marketing executive
- Media director
- Media executive
- Public relations director/specialist
- Wholesale sales representative

BUSINESS MANAGEMENT
- Apartment manager
- Caterer
- Convention center manager
- Executive housekeeper
- Funeral director
- Golf club manager
- Hotel manager/assistant
- Restaurant site selector
- Restaurant/food service manager
- Store manager
- Vehicle leasing manager

CONTRACTS/CLAIMS
- Advance agent
- Booking agent
- Claims adjuster
- Insurance claim examiner
- Leasing manager
- Professional athletes' agent

ORGANIZING
ACTIVITIES SUCH AS SCHEDULING, ORDERING, CHECKING

This group of jobs involves activities that ensure that details of the work environment are kept accurate and in good order. People who are successful in these occupations typically are methodical, neat, and structured in their approach. Thus, they are more comfortable operating the established, rather than establishing a new operation.

ADMINISTRATIVE DETAIL
- Clerical supervisor/office manager
- Financial aid counselor
- Legal secretary
- Probation officer
- Real estate clerk
- Secretary/office administrator
- Technical administrative assistant
- Vault cashier

MATHEMATICAL DETAIL
- Accounting clerk
- Bookkeeper
- Claims examiner
- Invoice control clerk
- Payroll clerk
- Tax clerk

FINANCIAL DETAIL
- Cashier
- Head teller
- Layaway clerk
- Ticket sales supervisor

ORAL COMMUNCATIONS
- Customer service representative
- Customer service supervisor
- Hospital admitting clerk
- Hotel clerk
- Receptionist
- Reservation agent
- Switchboard operator

RECORDS PROCESSING
- Copyright expert
- Court reporter
- Credit manager
- Electronic data processor
- Equipment operator
- Mail carrier
- Medical records technician
- Merchandiser
- Mortgage processor
- Proofreader

CLERICAL MACHINE OPERATION
- Computer operator
- Data input operator
- Data-coder operator
- Proof machine operator
- Typesetter
- Typist

CLERICAL HANDLING
- Checker
- File clerk
- Mailroom supervisor
- Money counter
- Office helper

MATHEMATICS/STATISTICS
- Actuary
- Chief information officer
- Computer programmer
- Computer science expert
- Computer systems analyst
- Database manager
- Information systems manager
- Investment banker
- Investment professional
- Management consultant
- Mathematician
- Network administrator
- Operations/systems research analyst
- Statistician

FINANCE
- Accountant
- Auditor
- Bank loan officer
- Bank manager
- Bank teller
- Corporate financial analyst
- Environmental accountant
- Financial institution examiner
- Financial planner
- Investments manager
- Purchasing agent
- Real estate appraiser
- Underwriter

REGULATIONS ENFORCEMENT
- Air pollution control inspector
- Animal cruelty investigation supervisor
- Chief bank examiner
- Director of consumer affairs
- Health care facilities inspector
- Immigration inspector
- IRS agent
- Pesticide-control inspector

MAKING
ACTIVITIES SUCH AS ASSEMBLING, REPAIRING, GROWING, OPERATING

This group prefers practical activities that are hands-on, where the results of work can be immediately seen. They are often rugged and physically strong. These people generally prefer achieving practical, tangible, or visible results, rather than theoretical or intellectual pursuits.

MANAGERIAL WORK: PLANTS/ANIMALS
- Farm manger
- Forestry manager
- Greenskeeper
- Rancher
- Wildlife control agent

GENERAL SUPERVISION
- Disease and insect control field inspector
- Forestry aide
- Lawn and tree service supervisor
- Poultry hatchery supervisor

ANIMAL TRAINING/SERVICE
- Animal keeper
- Blacksmith
- Dog groomer
- Race horse trainer

ELEMENTAL WORK: PLANTS/ANIMALS
- Fish hatchery worker
- Forester (worker)
- Horticultural worker
- Milking machine technician

MANAGERIAL WORK: MECHANICAL
- Quarry supervisor
- Sanitation superintendent
- Solid-waste management supervisor
- Transportation maintenance supervisor

ENGINEERING TECHNOLOGY
- Building inspector
- Drafter
- Pollution control technician
- Surveyor

CRAFT TECHNOLOGY (NOTE: this is a very large subgroup with hundreds of jobs.)
- Aircraft technician
- Appliance/power tool reparier
- Chef
- Dental lab technician
- Electrician
- Electromedical equipment repairer
- Electronic technician
- Piano technician
- Plumber
- Sheet metal worker
- Telephone repairer
- Tool/die maker

SYSTEMS OPERATION
- Operation supervisor, nuclear power plant
- Power plant operator
- Water treatment plant operator
- Waterworks pump-station operator

QUALITY CONTROL
- Bridge inspector
- Elevator examiner
- Log grader
- Truck safety inspector

LAND/WATER VEHICLE OPERATION
- Ambulance driver
- Food service driver
- Tow truck operator
- Truck driver

MATERIAL CONTROL
- Cloth finisher
- Laundry supervisor
- Meter reader
- Parts, order, and stock clerk
- Auto mechanic service manager
- Baker

CRAFTS
- Floor covering layer
- Plumbing and hydraulics mechanic

EQUIPMENT OPERATION
- Bulldozer operator
- Concrete mixing plant supervisor
- Crane operator
- Motor grader operator

ELEMENTAL WORK: MECHANICAL
- Baggage handler
- Bricklayer
- Jackhammer operator
- Janitor/housekeeper

PRODUCTION TECHNOLOGY
- Aircraft assembler
- Machine operator
- Ophthalmic laboratory technician
- Packaging technician

PRODUCTION WORK
- Garment manufacturing supervisor
- Machinist
- Office/business machine repairer
- Press operator

QUALITY CONTROL
- Clothing inspector
- Electronics inspector
- Exhaust emissions inspector
- Meat grader

ELEMENTAL WORK: INDUSTRIAL
- Injection/molding machine operator
- Paint mixer
- Poultry packing supervisor
- Textile worker

CHAPTER
7

PUTTING YOUR PATTERN TOGETHER

This chapter contains the *Action Plan Summary*. It will be the collecting place for the key items of information gleaned from your surveys.

As you fill in each section, you'll see another part of your pattern of talents and interests. When it is completed, you'll have a good picture of the unique design God has given you.

Hint: Since you likely will find many uses for this information, take your time, and be neat.

ACTION PLAN SUMMARY

A STEP-BY-STEP GUIDE

FOR UNDERSTANDING AND USING

YOUR SELF-ASSESSMENT RESULTS

ACTION PLAN

Jesus said, *"Therefore everyone who hears these words of Mine, and* **acts** *upon them, may be compared to a wise man"* (Matthew 7:24).

Your commitment to complete this Action Plan and act upon it will determine the ultimate benefit you receive from this workbook. Please fill it out <u>completely,</u> discuss it with someone who knows you well, and become accountable for follow-through.

I. PERSONALITY TENDENCIES *(refer to your Personality I.D., Chapter 3)*

List the most prominent strengths and weaknesses associated with your personality profile that apply to you (see Personality I.D, page P-20).

STRENGTHS:

1. _____
2. _____
3. _____
4. _____
5. _____
6. _____
7. _____

WEAKNESSES:

1. _____
2. _____
3. _____
4. _____
5. _____
6. _____
7. _____

Are you more _____ task-oriented or _____ people-oriented?

Are you more _____ reserved (introspective) or _____ outgoing in your actions?

Are you more of a _____ specialist or _____ a generalist in your approach to work?

II. ABILITIES *(refer to your Skills Survey, Chapter 4)*

List below the four **Job Skill** areas in which you have the most expertise. These may or may not be a good match for you (see Skills Survey, page S-2).

1.	**3.**
2.	**4.**

List your top nine **Transferable Skills** below (see Skills Survey, page S-7).

1.	**4.**	**7.**
2.	**5.**	**8.**
3.	**6.**	**9.**

List your top six **Self-Management Skills** below (see Skills Survey, page S-9).

1.	3.	5.
2.	4.	6.

III. WORK PRIORITIES (refer to Work Priorities Evaluation, Chapter 5)

A. Enter here the four abilities you want to use most in your work (Section I, page W-4).

1. _____
2. _____
3. _____
4. _____

B. Enter here the most important characteristics of your preferred work environment (Section II).

1. _____
2. _____
3. _____
4. _____

C. Enter the kinds of activities you enjoy most at work (Section III).

1. _____
2. _____
3. _____
4. _____

D. List the top four outcomes you value most (Section IV). These likely will be key components that provide meaning and purpose to your life and work.

1. _____
2. _____
3. _____
4. _____

IV. VOCATIONAL INTERESTS (refer to Vocational Interest Survey, Chapter 6)

List your top three interest groups and four occupations that you would like to investigate from each of these interest groups (see page V-11).

OCCUPATIONAL INTEREST GROUP I _____

    1. _____

    2. _____

    3. _____

    4. _____

OCCUPATIONAL INTEREST GROUP II _____

    1. _____

    2. _____

    3. _____

    4. _____

OCCUPATIONAL INTEREST GROUP III _____

    1. _____

    2. _____

    3. _____

    4. _____

STOP HERE FOR A WORD FROM YOUR FRIENDLY CAREER COUNSELOR.

All of the work you have done thus far on your self-assessment has been very informative, but you can't stop yet. If you are like most people, you probably don't have a definitive occupation at this point. You must now bring everything into focus in order to narrow your choices.

The final steps in carrying out your action plan will require some concentrated thought and effort on your part. You must **analyze** what you have learned thus far and **synthesize** it into some final conclusions.

Unfortunately, many who go through a career assessment stop here and fall short of being able to use fully what they have learned. You may ask, "Why would they do that?" The problem is, it requires hard thinking and some people would rather just skip it. Either they don't have the confidence they can do it, or they just are not willing to exert the mental energy. But the truth is, you are a unique person with a unique set of circumstances, and your input is vital to your career decision process. Pulling it all together may sound hard, but it's not. The following questions will lead you through the process.

V. GO BACK AND ANALYZE

> **ANALYZE:** to draw relationships among ideas or to compare and contrast.

1. It's time to analyze the three occupational groups you listed on the previous page. Write one sentence that explains what motivates you about each group.

   Group I _____

   _____

   Group II _____

   _____

   Group III _____

   _____

2. What do you see that is similar about these three groups? _____

   _____

3. What do you see that is different about them? _____

   _____

4. One of these three groups may focus more on your favorite leisure or volunteer activities than on your work. Is this true? _____ Which one? _____

5. Look back at your work priorities in Sections III A and C (Action Plan Summary, page A-3). Are your preferences oriented more toward:
   ____ people, ____ data, ____ things, ____ ideas?

VI. GO THE FINAL MILE AND SYNTHESIZE

> **SYNTHESIZE:** to combine parts to form a unique or complex whole.

1. Good scientists carefully research the available information and meticulously gather evidence. In addition, they must also "synthesize" all the facts, relevant data, and evidence to come up with workable conclusions or theories. You have discovered a great many insights about yourself and your career potential. Like the scientists, you must now "synthesize" the evidence into some concluding statements.

   a. *Who are you?*

   Write three to five sentences that summarize your **strengths** and **motivations,** based on all you have learned about your personality, abilities, values, and occupational interests.

   _____

   _____

   _____

   _____

b. ***What kind of work matches your pattern?***

In the space below, write a five- or six-sentence paragraph that summarizes and describes the type of work for which you are best suited. Incorporate insights from your pattern descriptions, personality interests, abilities, and work values. THE GOAL: you should be able to compare potential job descriptions with this paragraph to see if the job really matches you.

_____

_____

_____

_____

_____

c. ***Which specific occupations match your pattern?***

Now go back and review the occupations you listed in Section IV (Action Plan Summary, page A-4) and evaluate them in light of paragraph **b** above. Select six that seem to be the best match and list them below.

(1) _____ ( )   (4) _____ ( )

(2) _____ ( )   (5) _____ ( )

(3) _____ ( )   (6) _____ ( )

Based on the summary description of your strengths (a) and your concluding statement (b), which describes the work for which you are best suited, how well do each of these occupations match your pattern? Use the following criteria to evaluate each of the occupations you listed. Place the appropriate letter (a, b, c, or d) beside each occupation of this section.

(a) Don't know yet. I need to do more research on the nature of this occupation. I will use the Career Investigation Worksheet at the end of this section.

(b) Does not seem to be a good match. Will need to look for a related occupational area that uses more of my strengths.

(c) Generally a good match, but I will try to refine to a closer match.

(d) Seems to be a good match to my talents and is the type of work I would enjoy doing. I understand that more research will be needed to identify:

—if further training is needed.   —if further education is required.

—companies in this field.   —job possibilities in this field.

d. ***Based on what you know about your motivations and weak areas, what type of work settings and responsibilities would you like to avoid?***

1. _____   3. _____

   _____   _____

2. _____   4. _____

   _____   _____

Note: People who have the qualities to flourish in these settings are quite different from you and may be able to provide good counsel to help balance your thinking as you make career decisions.

VII. SPECIFIC STEPS OF ACTION

A. List three specific steps you will follow in the next week, in light of what you have learned thus far.

1. _____

   _____

2. _____

   _____

3. _____

   _____

B. List three career goals you will pursue in the next 3 to 9 months to ultimately become a better steward of your talents. *"But prove yourselves doers of the word, and not merely hearers who delude themselves"* (James 1:22).

1. _____

   _____

2. _____

   _____

3. _____

   _____

TO WHOM WILL YOU BE ACCOUNTABLE FOR THESE STEPS?

Name: _____

YOU NEED CAREER INFORMATION

Throughout history, successful people have realized the importance of having good information for decision making. Historically, armies have sought the high ground to overlook the terrain and gather intelligence. In modern times, we have used hot air balloons, reconnaissance aircraft, and satellites to gather information for military and weather forecasting purposes. In the same way, if you are in a job search you need broad, accurate, and up-to-date information to wage your career search campaign.

Get on the Internet

The Internet is a great place to get a view of what's happening on the cutting edge of the world of work. You can search for jobs, get résumé and career search tips, submit your résumé for review, or do research on a company you are considering.

If you have an Internet online service, such as *America On Line*, *CompuServe*, or *Prodigy*, check its career/job services. These companies typically provide proprietary services of their own as well as links to regular net sites. In *America On Line* be sure to check Christian Career Center—keyword: COCC.

There are several good books out now that explain how to use the Internet for job search. Three that we have used are *How to Get Your Dream Job Using the Web* by Shannon and Arthur Karl, *Hook Up, Get Hired!* by Joyce Lain Kennedy, and the current edition of *What Color Is Your Parachute* by Richard Nelson Bolles.

In addition, we have included below a short list of some of the sites that we have visited, along with a brief description of some of their services. Keep in mind that most secular sites are much like the newspaper want ads, so please don't hold us accountable for their content.

- **ASAE–Employment Links**

  Links you to hundreds of employment services.
  http://www.asae.org/jobs/

- **America's Employers**

  Includes job postings, company databases, résumé bank, and chat room.
  http://www.americasemployers.com

- **America's Job Bank**

  Provides excellent source of job listings with links to other job banks.
  http://www.ajb.dni.us/index.html

- **Career Magazine**

  Features a very readable site on career information, with job openings and a résumé bank.
  http://www.careermag.com

- **Career Mosaic**

  In addition to job openings and résumé posting, this site offers a variety of information, such as résumé writing, relocation tips, and market trends and forecasting.
  http://www.careermosaic.com/

- **CareerPath.com**

  Gives you the ability to search six major city newspaper employment ads.
  http://www.careerpath.com

- **Career Resource Homepage**

  Provides links to databases for universities, newsgroups, career placement centers.
  http://www.rpi.edu/dept/cdc/homepage.html

- **E.span Interactive Employment Network**

  Provides current job openings, résumé writing tips, and the *Occupational Outlook Handbook*.
  http://www.espan.com/

- **Intercristo**

  Is a Christian job search network that provides a quick ministry-related job-matching service for a nominal fee.
  http://www.jobleads.org

- **Job Center**

  Using their form, you can post a résumé to various newsgroups and their databases, and they will e-mail you job suggestions you're qualified for.
  http://www.jobcenter.com

- **JobQuest**

  Offers career information, in addition to the *Occupational Outlook Handbook*.
  http://www.jobquest.com/

- **Job Safari**

  Provides link to a large and useful index of companies with employment information.
  http://www.jobsafari.com

- **Job Show**

  Jeanine Graf features video interviews with human resource consultants who offer jobs on her radio/TV programs.
  http://www.jobshow.com

- **Job Web**

  Links jobs, job seekers, and job search information services, sponsored by the National Association of Colleges and Employers.
  http://www.jobweb.com/

- **The Monster Board**

  Allows you to create your résumé, submit it, and talk to human resource people. Also lists jobs and profiles companies.
  http://www.monster.com/

- **Not Just Bibles**

  Guides you to Christian resources on the Internet.
  http://www.iclnet.org/pub/resources/christian-resources.html

- **Occupational Outlook Handbook**

  Provides specific information on occupations and gives employment projections.
  http://stats.bls.gov/ocohome.htm

- **Online Career Center**

  Offers largest online job search resources, resume posting, and career information.
  http://www.occ.com/

- **What Color Is Your Parachute: Job Hunting Online**

  Dick Bolles provides up-to-date information to aid in your job search.
  http://washingtonpost.com/parachute

Go to the Library and Career Centers

Most libraries and career centers can provide you with information on occupations, career areas, and companies. They will generally have the *Occupational Outlook Handbook* and many other resources. *Occupational Outlook Handbook* also can be accessed through the Internet at http://stats.bls.gov/ocohome.htm.

Gain an Interview

At some point in your career search, you may need firsthand information about the details of a particular occupation or job. It would be very helpful if you could set up an interview with someone who is successfully and happily employed in that field. He or she could give you an objective look at what is needed to succeed, as well as the pros and cons of the career field.

Usually it is easiest to interview someone you know. If that isn't possible, try to get a friend to arrange such a meeting with an appropriate candidate. In any case, schedule an appointment and stick with the agreed-upon purpose of the interview. Don't use this interview to ask for employment.

The following Career Investigation Worksheet gives some suggested questions to ask in an interview.

Career Investigation Worksheet *

Name of Occupation _____

Sources of information

☐ *Occupational Outlook Handbook*
(Library and Internet http://stats.bls.gov/ocohome.htm)
☐ Parents/friends
☐ Someone involved in this type of work
☐ Counselor—school or career guidance
☐ Career guidance pamphlets (Career Guidance Center)
☐ Computerized information or guidance system (Career Guidance Center)
☐ Military recruiter
☐ Other _____

Questions you'll want to ask

1. What are the duties in this job? _____
_____
_____

2. What is the primary purpose, product, or desired results
of the specific job? _____
of the company/organization? _____

3. What strengths/abilities are most important in this occupational field?
Personality strengths: _____
_____

Abilities/Skills: _____
_____

4. What is the working environment like? (hours, location, outdoors, office) _____
_____
_____
_____

5. What is the typical salary in this occupation? _____

6. What is the employment outlook in this career field? _____

7. What kind of education/training is required?
☐ On-the-job training
☐ Apprenticeship
☐ One or two years vo/tech school or community college
☐ Two-year college degree/certificate
☐ Four-year college degree
☐ Graduate or professional school after four-year college

Preparing for this career field

8. How much will the education/training cost? _____
How will you pay for it? (check all that apply)
☐ Work full time, attend classes off hours
☐ Scholarship
☐ Co-op program
☐ Work part time
☐ Parents/family
☐ Loans (Generally not recommended except for a short period. It's better to pay as you go.)

* Make a copy of this worksheet for each career field you are evaluating.   *(Continued on next page)*

Career Investigation Worksheet *

9. What specific area/major would you need to study? _____

10. What are the names of three places where you could get these courses or this kind of education/training? _____
_____
_____

11. How motivated are you to pursue the preparation necessary to enter this occupation?
   ☐ Not motivated
   ☐ Somewhat motivated
   ☐ Very motivated

Evaluation

12. Is this occupation reasonable and realistic for you? Compare your strengths to the requirements of this field to see how well you match.

	POOR	FAIR	GOOD	EXCELLENT
Interest				
Skills/Abilities				
Work Priorities and Values				
Personality				
Affordable at this time				

13. Based on the answers you have given to the questions above, are you ready to pursue this occupation?
   ☐ Yes
   ☐ No

14. If the answer to Question 13 is Yes, use the form below to develop an action plan to begin your education/training or to actually plan your job search.
   • Enroll in courses.
   • Seek a part-time job in this field.
   • Prepare a résumé.
   • Develop a job search plan.
   • Develop a network of contacts.
   • Begin job search.

15. I will take the following actions.

ACTION	SCHEDULED DATE	COMPLETED
a.		
b.		
c.		
d.		
e.		
f.		
g.		

NOTES: _____
_____
_____
_____
_____
_____

* Make a copy of this worksheet for each career field you are evaluating.

CHAPTER
8

MAKING CAREER DECISIONS

With Chapter 7 completed, you should have a good picture of your talents and interests. Before you move ahead and begin using this information, pause for a moment and take stock of your situation. Experience has shown that asking questions is an effective way to help people gain a clear focus for their career planning. The following questions are the ones we would ask if we were going to provide you with career counseling. It's important that you take sufficient time to think through and write your answers. In doing so, you'll have to confront career and life issues that need to be considered before making further career decisions.

1. What do you do in your current (or most recent) occupation?

_____

_____

_____

_____.

2. How did you get involved in this occupation?

_____

_____

_____

_____.

3. What were the criteria for choosing this job?

_____

_____

_____

_____.

4. What do you like best about your job?

_____

_____

_____

_____.

5. What do you like least about your job?

_____

_____

_____

_____.

6. How would your employer evaluate your performance on the job? How would your fellow workers evaluate it?

_____

_____

_____

_____.

7. What has motivated you to go through the career planning process at this time?

_____

_____

_____

_____.

8. If you could develop your career over again, what would you do differently? Why?

_____

_____

_____

_____.

9. How will the insights gained from your previous career decisions affect your current decision-making process?

_____

_____

_____

_____.

10. If you are married, how does your spouse feel about your situation? What is his or her counsel?

_____

_____

_____

_____.

11. Are you in a significant spiritual struggle at this time? If so, have you shared this with your spouse, pastor, or a Christian friend?

_____

_____

_____.

12. Is it possible there are issues other than your occupation that are the source of your current concern? What are they?

_____

_____

_____

_____.

13. How would you rate your overall financial situation: gaining, just making ends meet, falling behind, in debt, or going under?

_____

_____

_____

_____.

14. How much of your desire for a career change is motivated by a desire to increase your income?

_____

_____

_____

_____.

15. If you are in a financial struggle or anticipate being in one, are you willing to take immediate action to get on a budget and cut out all unnecessary expenses in order to avoid further indebtedness?

_____

_____

_____

_____.

16. Which of the following will affect your career decisions?

_____ proximity to family   _____ current financial condition

_____ access to education/training   _____ effect on children

The questions above may highlight areas that need attention. Seek help as appropriate for any noncareer issues that might be affecting your career decisions.

There are many issues that affect career satisfaction. Typical examples of what can cause dissatisfaction on the job are job-talent mismatch, an unethical employer, spiritual problems, bitterness, or relational problems.

To further analyze your career situation, take time to examine the following chart and identify any root causes of career dissatisfaction that might be affecting you.

The Roots and Fruits of Job Dissatisfaction

Unhappy in work

Constant conflict

Complaining

Ignorance

Not enough money

Fearful

Impulsive

Craving power/ authority

Job mismatch

Bitter

Stubborn

No recognition

Not motivated

Lack of faith
Heb. 11:6

Greed
1 Tim. 6:9;
Luke 12:15

Slothfulness
Prov. 26:13-16

Lust for things
Hag. 1:5-6

Pride
Prov. 11:2;
16:18

Rebellion
Rom. 13:1-5

Sound Roots Produce Good Fruit

Most of us have tasted some of the bad fruits (consequences) of bad choices in our careers. But praise the Lord, He can redeem our lives and careers.

Take time to study the roots and fruits associated with job contentment.

The Roots and Fruits of Job Contentment

Peace with
coworkers
Rom. 12: 18-21

Rejoicing
Gal. 5:22;
1 Thess. 5:16-18

Fulfillment
2 Tim. 4:7-8

Using strengths
Matt. 25:21

Facilitate life
purpose
Eph. 2:10

Needs met
Phil. 4:19

A light for Jesus
Matt. 5:14-16

Expresses love
for God
Matt. 22:37

Blessings
to others
Gen. 12:2-3

Faith
Heb. 11:6

Filled with Spirit
Eph. 5:18

Submission
Rom. 13:1
Col. 3:22-24

Peace with God
Rom. 5:1

Walk in Spirit
Gal. 5:16, 25

A good name
Prov. 22:1

A steward's attitude
Col. 3:17

Meditate on
God's Word
Ps. 1

How Do You Define Success?

One of the main problems we all face in our career planning is that we have been taught a worldly (short-term, self-centered) definition of success. In order for you to dedicate your talents in service to the Lord you'll have to have a biblical view of success.

Answering the following questions will help you gain this biblical view.

The Apostle Paul Was a Failure by the World's Standards

1. What happened to Paul as a result of his work? (Acts 24:23, 27; Philippians 1:12–14)

_____

2. What fears did he experience in Asia? (2 Corinthians 1:8–9)

_____

3. What resulted from Paul's work in Philippi? (Acts 16:22)

_____

4. What was the religious leaders' response to Paul's work? (Acts 24:1; 25:2,15)

_____

Yet Paul Was Successful in His Work/Mission

5. How did Paul respond to the mission Jesus gave him? (Acts 26:19–23)

_____

6. How did Paul's encounter with the world of his day affect him? (Acts 26:19–23)

_____

7. What was the key to Paul's success? (Acts 26:22)

_____

Paul Provided a Good Model for a Biblical Attitude Toward Success

In Philippians 3:8–13 we see that he:
- vs. 8   counted all things as loss to know Christ (values);
- vs. 9   desired to be found in Him (purpose);
- vs. 10   desired to know Jesus, the power of His resurrection, and the fellowship of His sufferings (realistic, balanced view of life);
- vs. 12   defined his life purpose by Christ's purpose for him (values);

- vs. 13 kept his goal in focus by doing one thing above all else (priority);
- vs. 14 pressed on toward the goal (persistence).

What Determines Success?

From the lives of the apostle Paul and others in the Bible, we can see that success should be determined by whether a person is fulfilling his or her life purpose. We know that our mission, as Christians, is to have a personal relationship with Jesus Christ and reflect His love as we help others come to know Him.

Unfortunately, our society uses criteria like wealth, positions of influence, and the amount of leisure time a person has to evaluate success. We must avoid measuring ourselves by the world's standards.

At the same time, Christians need to recognize that a person can be successful by the world's standards and still be successful in God's eyes. Abraham, Joseph, and David are good examples of those who were blessed with success by following God's plan; yet, they kept their focus on Him and fulfilled their purpose.

As you embark on your new career direction, your definition of success will have a major influence on your career choices. The following are the questions you must answer.

What kind of success will bring joy, peace, and contentment?

_____

Who is the Source of my success?

_____

In what ways am I a success by the world's standards?

_____

In what ways am I a failure by the world's standards?

_____

Have I identified God's mission or calling for my life?

_____

In what ways am I a success in carrying out this mission?

_____

CHAPTER
9

DEVELOPING YOUR RÉSUMÉ

Your résumé is an extremely important document. It provides a well-thought-out, concise picture of you—the job seeker. It must communicate the following.

What	How
your objective, qualifications, experience, and accomplishments.	quickly, clearly, and accurately.

Your Résumé Is Your Sales Brochure

The résumé is your personal sales brochure, and its primary purpose is to convince someone to interview you for a job opening. Remember the following.

- You are the product the résumé is trying to sell.

- Résumés are designed to allow people to get to know you quickly and easily during your job search.

- Nobody likes to be reduced to a mere scrap of paper, but there's little choice if you want a job.

- Résumés are used at every level of the organizational world.

Writing Your Résumé

You'll find that writing a résumé takes a lot of mental effort. (The work sheets provided at the end of this chapter will help you to get started.) Most people will find it stressful work and want to quit before they really get a good product. Make a commitment to stay with it until it's right. Keep the following suggestions in mind.

- No one can write a top-notch résumé on the first try; you'll need to make several rough drafts.

- Your future employer needs to know your potential, so don't downplay your achievements. Ask someone to help you communicate the impact of your work.

- Your first draft should be as long as necessary to include all the relevant facts.

- Revise and edit to cut out every needless word. The hardest part of writing a résumé is figuring out how to present only the essentials—effectively.

- Your résumé must do its job in the first five to twenty seconds. That's the time you have to "catch the eye" of the decision maker.

The final product of your résumé should be

- limited to one page unless you have more than ten years of work experience—then keep it to two pages maximum.

- well-designed, informative, and internally consistent.

- airy looking. No one wants to read through huge blocks of solid type.

- high quality—both in content and appearance. Be sure it looks good. Laser printing is the standard.

Electronic Résumés

The use of electronic résumés is growing rapidly because they offer companies a quick, inexpensive way to screen large numbers of résumés. By scanning the paper version with an optical reader, companies can capture résumés into a database and electronically screen them via key word searches. Perhaps even more common is the posting of résumés through Internet job sites or submitting them via e-mail directly to the company (see Example #4–electronic version on page 84).

Tips for Contents: Key Words

Key words can be specific skills, education, salary expectation, companies you've worked for, titles, or whatever that company values most. Unlike the action verbs that used to get attention in the past, these keywords most probably will be nouns. For instance, if a company is looking for a computer software developer, they might search a file of résumés, looking for those that contain key words such as: *computer programmer, BS Computer Science, Visual Basic, Microsoft Access, C++, five years experience, Internet, Java, Web Browser, software development,* and *software manager.* The database search engine would rank résumés in the file based on the number of hits on these key words that were found in each résumé.

It is best to place the most important key words near the beginning of the résumé. In fact, it is not unusual for résumés today to contain a key word summary following the objectives. You would do well to learn more about the use of key words through Web sites or books (see those listed on page 118 at the end of Chapter 12).

One note of caution: When posting on the Internet, give only your name, phone number, and e-mail address. For security reasons, do not give your street address, business address, names of past employers, or references.

Tips for Creating an ASCII Résumé

In order to facilitate accurate scanning/reading by OCR (Optical Character Recognition) software, electronic résumés are typically developed and sent in ASCII format. This is a text only format. If you send your electronic résumé in another format without converting it to ASCII, it probably will be scrambled on the other end when it is converted. It is important to create a professional résumé that can be accepted electronically by anyone and that contains the elements that will be noticed.

ASCII files are not difficult to create, but they are more difficult to make interesting. The following tips should help.

- **Use a monospace font, such as Courier.**

  Times, Arial, and Helvetica fonts are proportionally spaced.

- **To create interest, use capital letters, spacing, and tabs.**

  Avoid formatting with bold, italics, underline, or graphics, since these are not captured by the scanner.

- **Keep each line less than 70 characters.**

  (example: `This line contains less than 70 characters and is in Courier font.`)

- **Use a font size between 10 and 14 point.**

- **Use a lowercase letter "o," an asterisk, or a hyphen for bullets.**

  (Be sure to leave at least one space between the bullet and your text.)

- **Save your completed résumé as an ASCII file.**

  (If you are in Word, save as Text Only. If you are in WordPerfect, save as DOS text.)

You may want to add this sentence at the end of your ASCII résumé: I have omitted certain personal information for security reasons and have formatted this in ASCII. A complete, attractive, and fully formatted hard copy version of this document is available upon request.

Résumé Formats

There are two primary formats for résumés that we recommend: **reverse chronological** and **functional.** (Examples of both are shown at the end of this chapter.) Small variations in format are acceptable, depending on the unique situation of the individual.

Generally, it's better to stick fairly close to the suggested formats; they are what employers are accustomed to seeing. The best way to develop your résumé is to look at some good models and then adapt them to your specific situation.

A. *Reverse Chronological Format.* (See Example #1 on page 81.) This format highlights your jobs and what you did in them and is especially good for showing a progression of responsibility. This résumé format might be preferred if you are staying in the same career field in which the job progression will be more obvious and relevant to the reader.

Remember that the reverse chronological résumé format is not just a laundry list of when and where you worked. The jobs should come alive and highlight the impact you had on the organization. Avoid using more space for old jobs than for recent ones.

Chronological Résumé

Name, address, phone and fax numbers
> This is vital information.

Career objective
> Briefly state your objective. How specific you should be depends on your career field and the breadth of the audience you are addressing with the résumé.

Employment history
> Begin with your latest employer and work backward. For a chronological résumé, this is where you detail any accomplishments and the impact they had on the company. Remember, it is not enough to say just what you did. Your résumé must specifically communicate your strengths and your achievements.

Education
> Again use the reverse chronological format to list your schools, locations, any degrees earned, and the graduation dates. Include any honors, such as "deans list" or "summa cum laude" or "Phi Beta Kappa."

(The following are categories you may or may not want to use, depending on your unique situation.)

Affiliations
> In this section you could list professional associations, certifications, or relevant nonprofit or Christian organizations of which you are a member.

Honors
> This is not included unless you have received exceptional or unusual honors that are not revealed in any other section of the résumé.

Personal
> Be careful with this one. Use this category only for information that you know will be relevant to the reader. Knowing your audience will be very important.

References available upon request
> Be certain you have references lined up before you send out résumés. More will be said about references later.

B. *Functional Résumé.* (See Examples #2 and #3 on pages 82 and 83.) If you haven't had an outstanding job progression, you have little experience, or you're changing career fields, you might want to consider this format. It will focus on the strengths you have to offer the company.

In the functional résumé you will use headings that focus on the skills you have that would apply to the job objective you are seeking. Use "bulleted statements" to highlight your experience and lend impact to the organizational layout. A bulleted statement is just an action-oriented statement that describes how you used or developed a skill in the past. Below are typical headings for a functional résumé.

Functional Résumé

Name, address, phone and fax numbers
This is vital information.

Career objective
Briefly state your objective, focusing on the types of activities you want to be involved in, rather than a specific job title. This makes the résumé more flexible.

Highlights of qualifications
List four or five of your strongest qualifications.

Relevant skills and experience
Give evidence of your three or four strongest skills—the ones you want to use in your work.

Employment history
Give a reverse chronological listing of your employment.

Education and Affiliations
Use reverse chronological format to list your schools, locations, degrees earned, and graduation dates. Include honors.

References available on request.

Strong Achievement Statements Are Important

The general appearance of your résumé gives the first impression of you. However, once the reader gets into your work experience, it's the impact of your accomplishments that will attract attention, so use strong verbs and verifiable facts as much as possible.

Following are some examples of how to describe achievements.

- Managed and maintained medical records of 1,200 patients for two doctors; received bonuses and letters of recognition five years successively for superior performance.

- Planned, organized, and supervised all activities for a banquet of 300 people.
- Increased regional sales by 12 percent, resulting in an increase of $42,000 net profit.
- Wrote operations manual, used by over 2,000 employees in three company plants.
- Opened and developed four accounts, which generated $420,000 in annual sales.
- Developed personal computer spreadsheets, pricing forms, and quarterly account sales reviews.
- Deployed and led a team of eight logisticians in providing on-time supplies to 4,000 soldiers during Operation Desert Storm.
- Highly proficient in Lotus, dBase IV, and WordPerfect: 60 wpm.

Effective Sentence Openers Create Impact

People who read and evaluate résumés are interested in results rather than activities, so be sure your résumé communicates what you've achieved.

The best way to communicate the results of your work is to use strong, direct, and positive-sounding words as sentence openers. A list of strong words is shown below. Remember you want to show your accomplishments, but always be totally honest and factual in your résumé.

Effective Sentence Openers

accelerated	developed	launched	reduced	summarized
accomplished	devised	led	reorganized	superseded
achieved	directed	maintained	replaced	supervised
activated	doubled	managed	researched	surveyed
added	eliminated	modified	responsible	systematized
administrated	established	negotiated	revamped	terminated
advanced	exceeded	obtained	saved	tested
approved	excelled	opportunity	scheduled	trained
assigned	expanded	organized	serviced	transacted
assisted	fabricated	originated	simplified	transferred
chose	formulated	participated	skilled	translated
completed	generated	performed	sold	trimmed
conceived	guided	planned	solved	tripled
conducted	hired	processed	spearheaded	turned
consolidated	identified	programmed	stabilized	uncovered
controlled	implemented	promoted	started	unified
coordinated	improved	proposed	strategically	unraveled
created	increased	purchased	streamlined	widened
decreased	initiated	recorded	strengthened	withdrew
delivered	installed	recouped	stretched	won
demonstrated	introduced	recruited	structured	wrote
designed	joined	redesigned	succeeded	

Check and Recheck Your Résumé

After you have checked your résumé thoroughly, and before taking it to the laser printer, have someone who is knowledgeable about résumés check it. Encourage that person to be tough, and don't be offended if he or she points out some problems. Keep in mind, you need every critique you can get; having a top quality résumé is your goal.

The following résumé checklist will help you and your critic catch many of your mistakes.

Résumé Checklist

1. Categories

Name, address, phone number(s)
Objective
Summary (Optional)
Professional experience or skills
    Dates
    Company name
    Job title
    Job description
        responsibilities
        duties
        achievements
Education
    Name of institution
    Degree(s)
    Years(s)
Other
    Professional memberships
    Awards
    Honors
    Publications

2. Format

Logically organized
Reverse chronology (where applicable)
Internal consistency
Appropriate amount of space for each entry

3. Layout

Margins
    external
    internal
Airiness
Easy readability
Eye-catching (underlining and use of capitalization)
Individualized (has a "personal touch")

4. General

Avoidance of abbreviations
    Inclusive of exact detail
    Sentences versus phrases (consistent use of one or the other)
Achievement-oriented

5. Proofreading

Spelling
Punctuation
Written style
    corrections
    naturalness
    clarity
    absence of cliches or business jargon

Use a Cover Letter

Use every opportunity to include a cover letter with your résumé. It enables you to relate directly with the person(s) who will be reviewing your résumé.

In your cover letter explain why you are contacting the recipient, and show how your talents might fit in that organization. Be sure you know something about the company, and tailor your comments to its particular needs.

The cover letter should be one page or less and businesslike, but it is much more personal than the résumé. A cover letter format is shown on page 80.

Line Up Your References

You normally provide references only when the potential employer asks for them. You should have them ready because you don't know when they will be needed. Before you send out any résumés, contact your references and get permission to use their names for reference.

Generally, references will come from three different groups of acquaintances.

1. Character references (people who know you well and can confirm or witness to your integrity and dependability).

2. Job performance references (previous supervisor or business colleague).

3. Professional expertise references (clients, peers, or competitors).

Identify several in each group, contact them by phone or letter, and ask if they are willing to be references. Be sure they understand your current employment situation and what you are seeking. Find out if these people would be comfortable giving you a good recommendation.

Refine your list of references to about two in each category and type their names and addresses on a single sheet in the same style and quality of printing as your résumé. Do not provide your reference list until an employer requests it.

Send a thank you note to your references, and also update them with the outcome of your situation.

RÉSUMÉ WORK SHEET

(Use work sheets like this to organize your work history. Then condense this information into impact statements for your résumé.)

REVERSE CHRONOLOGICAL FORMAT

Name_____

Address_____

City, State, Zip_____

Phone/Fax_____

Objective (For electronic résumé, add Summary and use key words.)

Work Experience

Company Name_____

Location_____

Dates of Employment_____

Title_____

Primary Responsibilities_____

_____

_____

_____

Accomplishments (Highlight skills you want to use.)

_____

_____

_____

Company Name_____

Location_____

Dates of Employment_____

Title_____

Primary Responsibilities_____

_____

_____

_____

Accomplishments

_____
_____
_____

Company Name_____
Location_____
Dates of Employment_____
Title_____
Primary Responsibilities_____

_____
_____
_____

Education

High school (List only if you have no college degree.)

_____
College/university_____
Dates_____
Degree(s) earned_____

College/university_____
Dates_____
Degree(s) earned_____

Affiliations (List only the professional organizations that apply.)

Organization_____
Position held_____
Organization_____
Position held_____

References available upon request

(Don't forget to include this.)

RÉSUMÉ WORK SHEET
FUNCTIONAL FORMAT

Name_____
Address_____
City, State, Zip_____
Phone/Fax_____

Objective (For electronic résumé, add Summary and use key words.)

_____
_____
_____

Highlights of Qualifications

(Indicate only skills and achievements that relate to your strengths and your job objective.)

_____
_____
_____
_____
_____

Relevant Skills and Experience

_____
_____
_____
_____
_____

Employment History

(Dates)   (Employer name and location)

_____   _____
_____   _____
_____   _____
_____   _____
_____   _____

78

Education and Affiliations

Education

High School _____

College/University _____

Dates _____

Degree(s) Earned _____

College/University _____

Dates _____

Degree(s) Earned _____

Affiliations (List only the organizations that apply.)

Organization _____

Position held _____

Organization _____

Position held _____

References Available Upon Request

COVER LETTER FORMAT

Your Name
Your Address
Your Telephone Number

Date

Contact Name (if available)
Title (if available)
Company
Address

Dear Mr./Ms._____:

Refer to the advertisement and/or position for which you are applying.

Identify that your background and education make you an excellent candidate for the position. Indicate and describe why your qualifications make you an ideal candidate for the position. Give one or two specific accomplishments that most effectively highlight your match for the job.

Identify 2 or 3 personal qualities that represent you as an employee and explain how those qualities might benefit the organization.

Express appreciation for the attention to your information and request an interview. Provide your contact information (phone numbers, times to call).

Sincerely,

(Signature: if your name is Susan, but you are called Sue, sign it Sue.)

Your Full Name (typed)
(as it appears on your heading)

Example #1

Thomas N. Williams
2314 Mountain View Dr
Yorba Linda, CA 92686
(714) 529-0297

OBJECTIVE: Responsibilities in management, marketing, or advertising in a growing company that offers a quality product and quality service.

EXPERIENCE:

1994—present   *Smartbucks Software Inc., Villa Park, CA*

1996   Director of Marketing—Responsible for sale of all company products; including international distribution. Increased sales by $900,000 in 1996 and led organization to a significant growth in product sales every year.

1994   Manager of Customer Support— Guided a staff of 18 service representatives in responding to orders, inquiries, and complaints. Processed/resolved over 2,400 actions per month.

1992—1994   *West Coast Financial Service, Tustin, CA*
                                 Sales Representative—Marketed mutual funds and insurance programs. Selected top salesman in district for 1993.

1990—1992   *SDI Communications, Riverside, CA*
                                 Account Executive II—Marketed long distance operations to businesses billing $2,500 to $25,000 per month. Won Directors Circle Award 1991.

1983—1990   *CleanStep Inc., Wheaton, IL*
                                 President—Owned and operated a carpet, upholstery, and drapery cleaning business. Expanded business to revenues of $120,000 annually. Sold business in October 1990 to move closer to aging parents.

1980—1983   *WMOT-TV (NBC Affiliate), Chicago, IL*
                                 Advertising Sales Representative

EDUCATION: B.S. Business Administration, 1980
                                 University of Illinois, Champagne, Urbana, IL
                                 Attended on football scholarship and was selected as all–conference wide receiver (1979).

                                 REFERENCES AVAILABLE UPON REQUEST

Example #2:
Katherine A. Wilson
1000 Chattahoochee Rd
Gainesville, GA 30550
(404) 999-4951

OBJECTIVE: Position in Administrative Services, with an opportunity for personal growth and career development.

HIGHLIGHTS OF ABILITIES
- Highly organized and detail-oriented
- Excellent communication skills
- Supportive team worker; committed and responsible
- Reliable and adaptable; learn new processes quickly; and take initiative

RELEVANT SKILLS AND EXPERIENCE

Office Experience
- Maintained folders and information for over 5,000 clients
- Operated a wide range of office machines, including copiers, printers, typewriters, and voice mail
- Processed incoming and outgoing mail

Telephone and Communication Skills
- Managed inbound and outbound call activities to include customer service
- Explained insurance policies to clients

Computer Knowledge
- Operate various software applications: word processing, databases, statistical testing analysis (IBM compatible)
- Process and scan test packages daily

EMPLOYMENT HISTORY

Present	Administrative Assistant	Mountainview Nursing Home, Gainesville, GA
1991–92	Administrative Assistant	World Insurance, Athens, GA
1991	Scoring Technician	Career Pathways, Gainesville, GA
*1989–91	Waitress/Event Organizer	Columns Country Club, Athens, GA
*1988	Packaging/Customer Assistance	Bigg's Grocery Store, Athens, GA
*1987–88	Children's Clothing Specialist	Mall Dept., Store, Athens, GA
*1986–87	Banquet Waitress	University of Georgia, Athens, GA
*1986	Cashier	Favers Dept., Store, Athens, GA

* Part-time jobs held during high school/college

EDUCATION

North Georgia College, Dahlonega, GA 1988–89, psychology major

REFERENCES AVAILABLE UPON REQUEST

Example #3:
                          Jane A. Smith
                          4110 Dogwood St
                          Berol, GA 30842
                          (404) 999-1919

OBJECTIVE: Writing/editing position, with opportunity to work with desktop
publishing systems

HIGHLIGHTS OF QUALIFICATIONS
- Over six years experience in the publishing field
- Reputation for accuracy in writing and editing
- Skilled in research and organization of written articles
- Highly conscientious worker with experience in meeting deadlines while
  maintaining quality

RELEVANT SKILLS AND EXPERIENCE

Write/Edit/Proofread
- Organized, developed, and wrote factual articles for three well-respected
  regional food industry publications
- Edited news releases and other submitted materials to a suitable size
- Proofread copy for publications
- Collaborated with production manager to be sure advertisements were
  produced to specifications, ensuring client satisfaction
- Completed proofreading workshop sponsored by Superior Builders

Research/Interview
- Conducted research for articles utilizing various print media
- Interviewed food industry executives both by telephone and in person as
  part of research for articles in *Computer Operation*
- Over three years experience on IBM personal computer, utilizing *WordStar*
  and *MicroSoft Word* word processing systems
- Trained on Macintosh *Quark Xpress* desktop publishing software system

EMPLOYMENT HISTORY

Detail Wrightsville Publishing Company, Inc.
Wrightsville, GA
March 1992–Present—Associate Editor
August 1988–February 1992—Business Writer/Reporter

1985, 86, 87 Summer Day Camp Counselor
Wrightsville Parks and Recreation Department
Wrightsville, GA

EDUCATION

A.B., English, University of GA, Athens, 1988. Summa cum laude, Phi Beta Kappa
A.A., Gainesville College, Gainesville, GA, 1986. Deans List.

Example #4:

Electronic Resume

JANE A. SMITH
4110 Dogwood St
Berol, GA 30842
(404) 999-1919

OBJECTIVE
       Writer/editor position, with opportunity to work with desktop
       publishing systems.

SUMMARY
Desktop publisher with ten years experience in publishing. Reputation for accurac
as writer, editor, and researcher. Skilled in organization of written articles.
Conscientious in meeting deadlines while maintaining quality. Highly proficient in
PageMaker 6.5 and Microsoft Word and PowerPoint with training on Macintosh Quark
Xpress desktop publishing
software.

RELEVANT SKILLS AND EXPERIENCE

Write/Edit/Proofread
*   Organized, developed, and wrote factual articles for three well-respected
regional food industry publications
*   Edited news releases and other submitted materials to a suitable size
*   Proofread copy for publications
*   Collaborated with production manager to be sure advertisements were produced
        to specifications, ensuring client satisfaction
*   Completed proofreading workshop sponsored by Superior Builders

Research/Interview
*   Provided research for articles, utilizing various print and electronic media
*   Conducted interviews of food industry executives both by telephone and in
person as part of research for articles in "Computer Operation"

EMPLOYMENT HISTORY
       March 1992-Present: Associate Editor
       August 1988-February 1992: Business Writer/Reporter
       Detail Wrightsville Publishing Company, Inc.
       Wrightsville, GA

       1985,86,87 Summer Day Camp Counselor
       Wrightsville Parks and Recreation Department
       Wrightsville, GA

EDUCATION
A.B., English, University of GA, Athens, 1988. Summa cum laude, Phi Beta Kappa
A.A., Gainesville College, Gainesville, GA, 1986. Deans List.

REFERENCES AVAILABLE UPON REQUEST

Note: I have formatted this in ASCII. A complete, attractive, and fully formatted
hard copy version of this document is available upon request.

CHAPTER
10
<hr>

ORGANIZING FOR THE JOB SEARCH

There probably isn't a person in the world who welcomes the task of looking for a job. Yet, it is a challenge most of us will encounter once, or possibly several times, during our working lifetime. If you are facing a job search, the concepts and strategies in this chapter will provide a sound methodology for a successful effort.

Step 1. Have a Positive Attitude

If you are looking for a job because you are unemployed, you may be experiencing one of the most difficult times of your life. If so, take a few minutes right now to read the four chapters of Philippians. Paul wrote this letter of encouragement while in prison, and his attitude can inspire us today just as it did his friends in Philippi 2,000 years ago.

Anyone involved in a job search definitely will need to be inspired, because the most important element of your search will be your attitude. You also must believe that your attributes are needed in the workplace. You must believe that there's a place where you can find meaningful employment that will allow you to fulfill your calling.

Attitudes affect how one person relates to others. Many employers and people in your network are going to read you like a book; so, even if you've received more than your share of raw deals, you still must love and have a positive attitude toward others. If you are harboring bitterness, turn it loose before it eats into you and destroys your opportunity to land the job that fits you.

To further set your attitude in the right direction, read the four axioms that are critical to the successful job search.

a. *Campaigns are rarely won in one battle.* You should plan from the start for the long haul. Take time to map a strategy that will carry you through to success whether it comes in two weeks or two years.

The following diagram depicts a mind-set that will allow you to learn from your mistakes and improve your tactics.

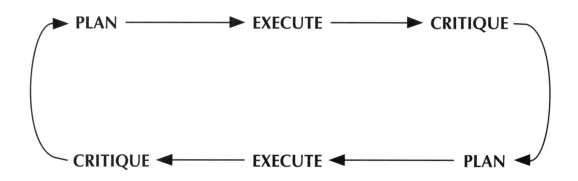

b. *Victory ultimately comes from the heart.* The person who is truly committed to winning usually does.

c. *God is sovereign over all.* Believers may not get what they want, but if they allow God to work in their lives they will get what is best for them.

d. *Our role is to faithfully work the process and trust God for His results.* When you decide on the results, you limit His blessing. His results are always better than what you would have anticipated.

Axioms **a** and **b** above prescribe our responsibilities, and **c** and **d** describe God's role. It seems He has designed this world to operate as a partnership. The good news is that we have a Partner who will never let us down.

The following chart reflects the concepts in the axioms and graphically depicts an important principle in career decision making. As you begin your job search, focus on carrying out a diligent, intelligent, Christ-honoring process, and let Him take care of the results.

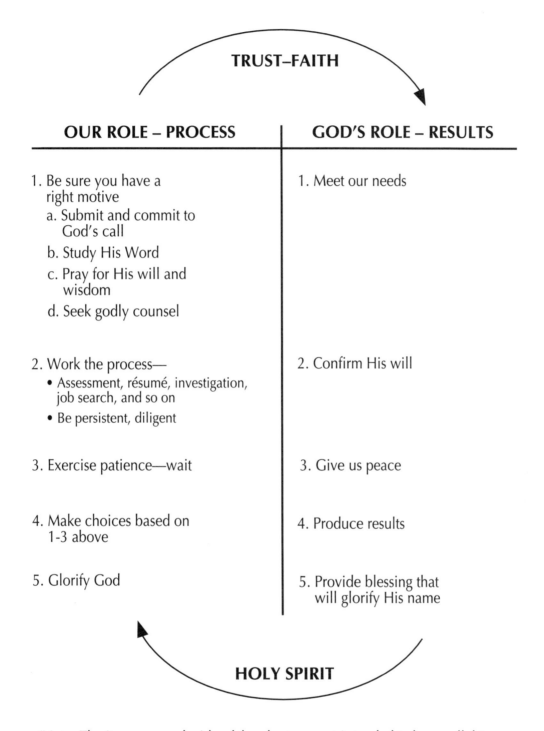

TRUST–FAITH

OUR ROLE – PROCESS	**GOD'S ROLE – RESULTS**

1. Be sure you have a right motive
   a. Submit and commit to God's call
   b. Study His Word
   c. Pray for His will and wisdom
   d. Seek godly counsel
	1. Meet our needs

2. Work the process—
   • Assessment, résumé, investigation, job search, and so on
   • Be persistent, diligent
	2. Confirm His will

3. Exercise patience—wait	3. Give us peace
4. Make choices based on 1-3 above	4. Produce results
5. Glorify God	5. Provide blessing that will glorify His name

HOLY SPIRIT

(Note: The items on each side of the chart are not intended to be parallel.)

Step 2. Join a Support Group

A job search can be a scary experience. A Christian support group can provide encouragement, information, techniques, network, contacts, and opportunities for spiritual growth. Check the announcement section of your local paper for meeting times. If a group is not available in your community, consider starting one.

Step 3. Determine Your Objective

You need a focus for your job search and it should be based on your talents, interests, and experience. Be sure you can communicate your objective clearly to those you meet. You may need an interim objective just to get your foot in the door or to get started.

Step 4. Develop Your Résumé

Your résumé should focus on your objective. Be sure it identifies the skills that qualify you for the objective.

Step 5. Maximize Your Network

The experts say that only about 15 to 20 percent of all job openings are ever advertised. Most are filled by hiring someone the employer knows or someone who has networked to the employer. If you stop and think about it, this makes sense because you would rather hire someone who is known rather than unknown.

Your goal should be to get every person who knows you to network your name to potential employers. We recommend you make network lists by category and then let others know your situation, as well as how they might help you.

Some of the categories in which you would already have a network are: family and friends, customers and clients, professional associations, previous employers, community contacts, service club acquaintances, and boards and committees on which you serve. You also should consider how you might expand your network by volunteering in your church and community.

Be very considerate of the people in your network. Don't ask them to do something they can't do. Generally, you are asking them for their input into your situation, due to their experience, knowledge, or position.

Use the phone and contact letters to establish your contacts and to follow up as necessary. A sample contact letter format and contact tracking log are located at the end of this chapter.

Step 6. Pursue Various Job Leads and Sources

Read the classified ads in Sunday papers, specialty papers, and professional journals. Also consider temporary employment. Basically you want to consider every opportunity for employment.

Step 7. Make Your Job Search Your Job

Establish a work schedule of 40 hours a week; set up an office somewhere and get organized; set goals and be accountable for your progress; and try to meet with two potential employers each day.

Step 8. Keep Your Life in Balance

During this stressful time, you need to attend to your spiritual, physical, and emotional needs. Spend time with God in prayer, Bible study, and devotions. Schedule time with your family, and perhaps do some special projects around the house to gain a sense of accomplishment.

Regular exercise, such as walking, is especially important for stress relief and good health. Don't feel guilty about scheduling some leisure activities.

Finally, be sure to reach out to others who are in need. When we get involved in helping others, it takes our focus off our own problems and puts them in a more balanced perspective.

Step 9. Consider Alternative Sources of Employment

To earn income while searching for a job, many people are able to use their skills and experience in consulting. Some will decide to change career fields entirely, and this will open up some totally new possibilities.

A few people will start their own businesses as a result of being unemployed. If you are considering this avenue, be sure to read Chapter 12 before you begin your career as an entrepreneur.

Step 10. Prepare for the Job Interview

Research the company, its products, and its leadership team before your interview. Rehearse your interview with someone you know, then with someone you don't know, so you will be prepared to be questioned by a stranger. (Some typical interview questions are given on page 93.) This will give you confidence under pressure.

To be sure you are completely ready for your interview, have a plan so that everything leading up to the appointment will go smoothly. Some items to check:

a. Pay attention to your appearance. Look neat and be appropriately dressed.

b. Have transportation ready in advance. Clean your car inside and out and fill it with gas. This is a confidence booster.

c. Get directions and make a trip to the interview location to be sure you know the way and where to park.

d. During the interview, be cordial, confident, and cautious about what you say, but be enthusiastic. Keep your responses to the point.

e. Follow up your interview with a letter, as shown at the end of this chapter.

Step 11. Negotiate the Job and Find out the Details

Try to find out in advance as much as possible about the company's normal policies and typical benefits. This way you know what to expect and can discuss them intelligently.

In your discussions with the decision maker and the personnel department, find out the basic info you will need to know.

starting date_____supervisor_____

hours_____written job description_____

working relationships (supervisors)_____

travel expected_____dress code_____

benefits_____work site_____

relocation allowance_____starting pay_____

advancement_____employee policy manual_____

Ask for an offer of employment in writing, and agree on a time by which you should reply. Don't consider the offer final until you actually go to work. For that reason, don't release your other options until you begin the new job.

Be sure all contingencies, such as physical exams and security clearance, are covered.

Step 12. Begin Preparing for the Next Job

Since most of us can expect to make a job shift, either within the company or to an entirely different company, you should always be preparing for the next job.

The best way to prepare is to develop your skills, care about your work, and excel in it. Others will notice, and your expertise and commitment will become known. In today's changing world, you can't afford to sit still and let opportunities pass by; so keep abreast of your field, and continually broaden your knowledge.

Expand your network of associates within and outside your company and field. Remember what we said earlier about networking. It's the way most positions are filled. The greater your network, the better your opportunities for making a smooth transition to your next job. Your goal is to have skills, experience, and network contacts so well established that people will be asking you to come work for them.

COVER LETTER FORMAT
(Network follow-up)

1420 Glenview Rd
Brentwood TN 37027
January 5, 19—

Mr. John Archer
Vice President, Marketing Division
Petro Oil Inc
147 Tacoma Pl
Toledo OH 54321

Dear Mr. Archer: (Or, use first name when possible.)

As you suggested during our telephone discussion yesterday, I am enclosing two copies of my résumé.

My goal is to become project manager of a medium-sized chemicals firm. I have almost 20 years of experience in process design, cost, and on-site construction engineering. My work has taken me to numerous parts of the world and involved me in many types of processes, mostly in petrochemicals. I believe I can contribute most effectively in a medium-sized company where there is a real need for a broad-based generalist.

I have BSChemE and MsChemE degrees from the University of Tennessee and have taken accounting and organizational behavior courses in Vanderbilt's Owen MBA program. I have supervised as many as 50 people on recent $40 to $80 million projects in Tennessee and Canada. I will relocate and travel if required.

I look forward to hearing from you if you have any suggestions along the lines I've described above.

Sincerely,

Ralph Brown

Enclosure

CONTACT TRACKING LOG

Date	Contact Name	Situation	Action Taken	Follow-up	Outcome/ Future Action

TYPICAL INTERVIEW QUESTIONS

Having a good understanding of how you are going to answer specific questions is crucial to presenting your unique background, knowledge, skills, and abilities to a prospective employer.

Shown below are some "hypothetical," often-asked interview questions for your review and for which you need to prepare written answers. Writing your answers will allow you to formulate your thoughts and ideas better. It also will provide a quick and easy way to review and refresh your memory prior to your interviews. Study each question before you start jotting down your answers, and do not underestimate its potential difficulty.

1. What were your duties, responsibilities, and accomplishments in your last job? (Be specific and show that you know what you're talking about. If your last job was not related to the job for which you are interviewing, answer the question, then relate your most recent job that does apply.)

2. Briefly describe your educational background. (Answer all questions the way they're asked. When an interviewer says *briefly*, that's what is meant.)

3. Would you briefly summarize your work history? (Again, answer the question—be specific, but not wordy.)

4. Why are you leaving your current job? Or . . . Why are you interested in a new position at this time? (Give an answer that does not reflect negatively on you, the company, or other individuals.)

5. Tell me about yourself. Or . . . Give me a thumbnail sketch of yourself. (Have a concise response ready. Exactly what you say is not usually as important as providing a clear, orderly, and logical response. Avoid rambling and needless detail.)

6. What are your career goals? (Phrase your response in a way the potential employer can relate to.)

7. What do you consider your major assets? Or . . . What are your strengths? (This isn't a time for you to be overly modest. Present your assets with assurance.)

8. Do you have any weak points? Or . . . What are your weaknesses? (Everybody has some, but indicate only something that has positive implications. For example, "Because I want to see a job done correctly, I tend to be somewhat of a perfectionist.")

POST INTERVIEW FOLLOW-UP
LETTER FORMULA

Your Name
Your Address
Your Telephone Number

Date

Contact Name
Title
Company
Address

Dear Mr./Ms._____:

Identify the position for which you were interviewed and the date. Thank the interviewer for his or her time and the interview opportunity.

Express your interest in the position and the company. Refer to specific qualifications you have that will benefit the company and target any specifics that may have been discussed in the interview.

Close with a suggestion for another meeting, if applicable, and/or a reference to a follow-up call in a designated time period. Provide your contact information (phone number, times to call). Repeat your appreciation.

Sincerely,

(Signature: if your name is William, but you are called Bill, sign it Bill.)

Your Full Name (typed)
(as it appears on your heading)

CHAPTER
11

MANAGING YOUR FINANCES

We believe you should be a good manager of the resources God has entrusted to you. The Bible provides the principles that will enable you to have financial freedom. The foundation for being good stewards is to recognize that God owns it all and we manage it for Him.

Since Larry has provided instruction on these principles in a number of books and workbooks, as well as audio and video materials, the discussion in this chapter will be limited to a brief overview of good financial management.

Financial Freedom Allows Career Freedom

Every day we hear from people who would like to make a career change but can't because they are handcuffed financially. The vast majority of Americans live a lifestyle that takes everything they make just to keep their heads above water. One missed paycheck or even a decrease in earnings for a short period of time puts them under. Even worse, some are so deeply in debt they have to work two jobs just to keep up with payments.

All of us can be taken down financially when we encounter unexpected emergencies, such as serious illnesses or natural disasters. However, most people get themselves in bondage out of indulgence, ignorance, or both.

Your goal should be to become a good manager of what you have. That means to live a lifestyle in which your income exceeds your outgo, and you have something left over with which to build a surplus.

The typical family does not plan ahead and has to borrow for every "unexpected emergency," such as car repair, the birth of a child, or a trip to the emergency room. Without a surplus to cover the events that occur in every family, you'll never be able to catch up long enough to get out of debt and get ahead.

Financial Freedom Requires Commitment

Contrary to what most people think, the issue is not how much you make but how committed you are to living within your income—even to the point of spending less than you make so you can generate a surplus.

We can't emphasize enough the importance of making a total commitment to become debt free. God takes pleasure in keeping His commitments and He seems to have a special place in His heart for people who keep their commitments.

For example, a typical situation might involve a husband and wife who accumulated several thousand dollars in consumer debt. They become convicted that their debt and lifestyle are not consistent with God's will for their lives, and they make a commitment to Him to get out of debt. They arrange a meeting with a Christian Financial Concepts budget counselor and, soon, they have set up a budget.

As this couple begins to bring their spending under control, they also find that God intervenes in their lives by making their money go farther and by bringing in unanticipated funds.

Rather than spend their "windfall," they pour it into one of their high-interest debts. They pay it off and then take what they were paying on that debt to double up on their next similar obligation. They pay the second debt off and then take what they were paying on the other accounts to pay off the next debt.

If they continue to do this, the impact of their commitment is almost unbelievable. Within a relatively short time (usually 18 to 36 months) they are debt free. Then they can take all their debt reduction payments and create a surplus in a savings account.

Have a Goal of Being Debt Free

Good budgeting enables you to live within your income. If you are not able to live on what you have, the only alternative is borrowing, which puts you back in the hole.

Many people think that they can have more by borrowing, but the math shows you will always have less. When you borrow, you have to pay interest that might have been used to pay for something else.

We can't encourage you enough to make a commitment to become debt free and to build a surplus. These steps will allow you to have peace about your finances and free you to pursue career fields that pique your interest and utilize your strongest talents. As you achieve financial freedom, you will be able to choose your occupation with your heart rather than because of your financial needs.

The following testimony we received in a letter shows the wisdom of good financial planning.

"Because of following CFC's budget plan for many years, we had our finances in order. So, we knew how much we needed to live on while my husband was in school and we also knew if we could afford to live on a policeman's salary. Through God's leading, my husband graduated from the police academy this past December and is now working as a police officer and loves it!"

Take a Realistic Look at Your Income

To become a good manager of your finances, it's important to get an accurate reading on your income and outgo.

First, you must analyze your income. If you look at your pay stubs, you'll notice that your take-home pay is much less than what you earn. Withholding taxes (federal income tax, Social Security, Medicare, and state income tax) will account for 13 to 25 percent of your gross income. Be sure your withholding is adequate, and if you are self-employed don't get behind in your quarterly payments.

Take a realistic look at any other sources of income and be sure you don't overestimate their contribution to your cash flow. Remember, any windfall you get is added to the top of your earnings and will be taxed at your highest marginal tax rate.

An Irregular Income Invites Disaster

If you have an irregular income, such as a commission or seasonal income, you must figure an average projection for the year and divide by 12 to determine your average monthly income.

If your income varies, save money in the good months so you will have a surplus when the income drops off. You then draw a specific monthly salary from your deposits rather than spend all that comes in.

Once you have considered all the sources, determine your gross income and subtract your withholding taxes.

Gross income equals $_____.

Taxes equal $_____.

Set Aside Your Tithe

Your desire to honor God with at least 10 percent of your income is not only a form of worship; it reflects your trust that He is sufficient for all of your needs. If you are not in the habit of tithing, we encourage you to make a commitment to do so.

Tithe equals $_____.

By taking your total monthly income and subtracting your taxes and tithe, you will come up with a figure we call *Net Spendable Income* or *NSI*. Our budgeting program is based on percentages of *NSI*, because that reflects how much you actually have to work with each month.

Gross income minus taxes and tithe equals *Net Spendable Income (NSI).*

Gross Income		$_____
Tithe	$_____	
Taxes	$_____	
Total	$_____	$_____

Subtract tithe plus taxes from gross to get NSI. $_____

Identify How You Are Spending Your Money

Start keeping records on every penny you spend and track it by category and even by subcategory. The categories we use are shown in the budget form in this chapter. (See Form 1.)

To get a good idea of your variable expenses, such as medical care and car repair, look at your records for the past year or two. Divide a one-year total by 12 to get a good monthly average of how much you need to set aside. (See Form 2.)

Once you've determined your current spending in each of the categories, determine the recommended amount for your income level using the Percentage Guide for Family Income (Figure 11.1) and Form 3.

To get your percentage of *Net Spendable Income* for a category:

Divide your current category spending amount ＿＿＿＿＿＿
by your *Net Spendable Income.*   ＿＿＿＿＿＿

Compare Your Spending to the Guideline Budget

Use Figure 11.1 and Form 4 to compare your percentages to the guideline budget (Figure 11.2). **Keep in mind:** *The guideline percent (for your income bracket) multiplied by your NSI equals the recommended amount for your income level.*

For example, if you make $35,000 per year, your *NSI* is $2,071 per month. The guideline budget recommends 34 percent for Housing; so, if you stick to this amount, you would allocate $704 per month for *all* your housing costs.

Of course, we know that in many areas of the country that will be difficult to do, but keep in mind that if you spend more on one category, the amount in another category must decrease. You'll always be faced with choices on how to allocate your income. The advantage of a budget is that it enables you to see up front how increased spending in one category will affect what you have left to spend in other categories.

The *guidelines* are just that, and you should tailor your percentages to your personal situation. However, for average families, the guideline budget will be very close to the maximum you can afford to spend.

Most families get in trouble by spending too much on housing. Likewise, many single young people get in trouble spending too much on automobiles and entertainment.

Develop Your New Budget

Once you've analyzed your spending, you'll have to make choices. Rest assured that everyone struggles with this, and no matter how much you make you'll never seem to have enough to budget for everything you want. A budget will help you plan for your needs and help you prioritize your spending.

A budget is a living document, so expect to make adjustments from time to time. Initially you may have to make several changes as reality redefines your estimates, but after a year or two you'll fall into a pattern and only need minor updates.

When you make adjustments, your total spending still must not exceed your *NSI*. Think of it as a pie: No matter how you slice it, you've only got so much; if one slice gets bigger, another slice gets smaller.

Remember, if you spend more than 100 percent of your NSI, you will be operating in the red and your debt load will increase.

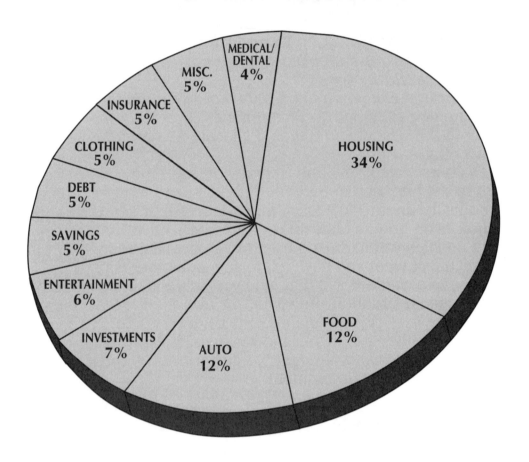

$35,000 ANNUAL INCOME FAMILY OF FOUR
Based on Net Spendable Income (NSI)

MEDICAL/ DENTAL 4%

MISC. 5%

INSURANCE 5%

CLOTHING 5%

DEBT 5%

SAVINGS 5%

ENTERTAINMENT 6%

INVESTMENTS 7%

AUTO 12%

FOOD 12%

HOUSING 34%

NSI=GROSS MINUS ALL TAXES AND TITHE

Establish Control Systems to Keep from Overspending Your Budget

Once your budget is set up, you'll have an opportunity to test your true faith and commitment. Making your budget work probably will require good control systems and some sacrifices. When you feel you are sacrificing, look around; you will see plenty of people living on less than you have. If you really want to appreciate how much you have, just look at how people in other countries live; you'll see that almost no one in the United States really has to sacrifice to live. Just remember, God knows your situation and will honor your commitment.

100

Now Is the Time to Start Living on a Budget

Knowing the minimum you need to live on will be important immediately if you lose your job. In that case, you should switch to a bare-bones budget and preserve any surplus to depend on during your job search. Having a good working budget will help you to know exactly where you stand and how long you can go without additional income.

In summary, to be a good financial manager, you will need to determine how much money you really need to live on, make a commitment to live within your means, get out of debt, and build a surplus. Based on our experience, living on a budget may be the most important step you could ever take to enhance your career opportunities.

As stated earlier, this chapter is primarily to give you a general idea of how to keep up with the income and outgo of your finances. Some sample budget forms are included so you can see how the concept works.

Other resources are available at your local Christian bookstore, or for more information on budgeting aids, as well as free information on career and financial management, call the Christian Financial Concepts toll free number at the end of this book or check the Christian Financial Concepts Web site at www.cfcministry.org. Ask about the *How to Manage Your Money* tape series and the budget notebook, *The Financial Planning Organizer*. We also have a budgeting software called *Money Matters*.

PERCENTAGE GUIDE FOR FAMILY INCOME
(Family of Four)

Gross Income	15,000	25,000	35,000	45,000	55,000	65,000
1. Tithe	10%	10%	10%	10%	10%	10%
2. Taxes [1]	<8%>	13%	19%	20%	21%	25%
NET SPENDABLE [2]	14,700	19,250	24,850	31,500	37,950	42,250
3. Housing	38%	38%	34%	30%	27%	26%
4. Food	15%	12%	12%	12%	11%	10%
5. Auto	15%	15%	12%	12%	12%	11%
6. Insurance	5%	5%	5%	5%	5%	5%
7. Debts	5%	5%	5%	5%	5%	5%
8. Ent./Recreation	4%	5%	6%	6%	7%	7%
9. Clothing	4%	5%	5%	5%	6%	6%
10. Savings	5%	5%	5%	5%	5%	5%
11. Medical/Dental	5%	5%	4%	4%	4%	4%
12. Miscellaneous	4%	5%	5%	7%	7%	8%
13. School/Child Care [3]	10%	8%	6%	5%	5%	5%
14. Investments [4]	—	—	7%	9%	11%	13%
15. Unalloc. Surplus Inc. [5]	—	—	—	—	—	—

[1] Guideline percentages for tax category include taxes for Social Security, federal, and a small estimated amount for state, with only the standard deduction taken. At the $15,000 level of income, the earned income credit drastically reduces the tax burden and produces a sizeable refund.

[2] Begin figuring 100% from this figure, not from Gross Income. Categories 3-12 (and 14 in higher income brackets) should add up to 100% of Net Spendable Income.

[3] This category is added as a guide only. If you have this expense, the percentage shown must be deducted from other budget categories.

[4] This category is used for long-term investment planning such as college education or retirement.

[5] This category is used when surplus income is received. This would be kept in the checking account to be used within a few weeks; otherwise, it should be transferred to an allocated category.

Figure 11.1   © Christian Financial Concepts, Inc. 5/96

BUDGET PERCENTAGE GUIDELINES

Salary for guideline = $35,000/year[1]

Gross Income per Month $2917

1.	Charitable gifts	(10% of Gross)	(2,917) =	$	292
2.	Taxes	(19% of Gross)	(2,917) =	$	554

Net Spendable Income (2,071)

3.	Housing	(34% of Net)	(2,071) =	$	704
4.	Food	(12% of Net)	(2,071) =	$	248
5.	Auto	(12% of Net)	(2,071) =	$	248
6.	Insurance	(5% of Net)	(2,071) =	$	104
7.	Debts	(5% of Net)	(2,071) =	$	104
8.	Enter./ Recreation	(6% of Net)	(2,071) =	$	124
9.	Clothing	(5% of Net)	(2,071) =	$	104
10.	Savings	(5% of Net)	(2,071) =	$	104
11.	Medical	(4% of Net)	(2,071) =	$	83
12.	Miscellaneous	(5% of Net)	(2,071) =	$	104
13.	School/ Child Care	(% of Net)	( ) =	$	
14.	Investments	(7% of Net)	(2,071) =	$	144
		100%		$ 2,071	

Total (Cannot exceed Net Spendable Income)

15.	Unallocated Surplus Income	(N/A) =	$	

[1] Refer to Figure 11.1 for percentage guidelines.

MONTHLY INCOME AND EXPENSES

GROSS INCOME PER MONTH _____
    Salary _____
    Interest _____
    Dividends _____
    Other _____

LESS:
  1. **Tithe** _____

  2. **Tax** (Est. - Incl. Fed., State, FICA) _____

    NET SPENDABLE INCOME _____

  3. **Housing** _____
    Mortgage (rent) _____
    Insurance _____
    Taxes _____
    Electricity _____
    Gas _____
    Water _____
    Sanitation _____
    Telephone _____
    Maintenance _____
    Other _____

  4. **Food** _____

  5. **Automobile(s)** _____
    Payments _____
    Gas/Oil _____
    Insurance _____
    License/Taxes _____
    Maint./Repair/Replace _____

  6. **Insurance** _____
    Life _____
    Medical _____
    Other _____

  7. **Debts** _____
    Credit Card _____
    Loans/Notes _____
    Other _____

  8. **Enter./Recreation** _____
    Eating Out _____
    Baby-sitters _____
    Activities/Trips _____
    Vacation _____
    Other _____

  9. **Clothing** _____

 10. **Savings** _____

 11. **Medical Expenses** _____
    Doctor _____
    Dentist _____
    Drugs _____
    Other _____

 12. **Miscellaneous** _____
    Toiletries, cosmetics _____
    Beauty, barber _____
    Laundry, cleaning _____
    Allowances, lunches _____
    Subscriptions _____
    Gifts (incl. Christmas) _____
    Cash _____
    Other _____

 13. **School/Child Care** _____
    Tuition _____
    Materials _____
    Transportation _____
    Day Care _____

 14. **Investments** _____

    TOTAL EXPENSES _____

INCOME VERSUS EXPENSES
    Net Spendable Income _____
    Less Expenses _____

 15. **Unallocated Surplus Income** [1] _____

[1] This category is used when surplus income is received. This would be kept in the checking account to be used within a few weeks; otherwise, it should be transferred to an allocated category.

FORM 1

VARIABLE EXPENSE PLANNING

Plan for those expenses that are not paid on a regular monthly basis by estimating the yearly cost and determining the monthly amount needed to be set aside for that expense. A helpful formula is to allow the previous year's expense and add 5 percent.

	Estimated Cost		Per Month
1. VACATION	$ _____	÷ 12 =	$ _____
2. DENTIST	$ _____	÷ 12 =	$ _____
3. DOCTOR	$ _____	÷ 12 =	$ _____
4. AUTOMOBILE	$ _____	÷ 12 =	$ _____
5. ANNUAL INSURANCE	$ _____	÷ 12 =	$ _____
(Life)	($ _____	÷ 12 =	$ _____)
(Health)	($ _____	÷ 12 =	$ _____)
(Auto)	($ _____	÷ 12 =	$ _____)
(Home)	($ _____	÷ 12 =	$ _____)
6. CLOTHING	$ _____	÷ 12 =	$ _____
7. INVESTMENTS	$ _____	÷ 12 =	$ _____
8. OTHER	$ _____	÷ 12 =	$ _____
	$ _____	÷ 12 =	$ _____

FORM 2

BUDGET PERCENTAGE GUIDELINES

Salary for guideline = _____ year[1]

Gross Income per Month _____

1.	Tithe	(10% of Gross)	(_____)	= $ _____
2.	Tax	(__ % of Gross)	(_____)	= $ _____

Net Spendable Income   _____ NSI

3.	Housing	(__ % of Net)	(_____)	= $ _____
4.	Food	(__ % of Net)	(_____)	= $ _____
5.	Auto	(__ % of Net)	(_____)	= $ _____
6.	Insurance	(__ % of Net)	(_____)	= $ _____
7.	Debts	(__ % of Net)	(_____)	= $ _____
8.	Entertainment & Rec.	(__ % of Net)	(_____)	= $ _____
9.	Clothing	(__ % of Net)	(_____)	= $ _____
10.	Savings	(__ % of Net)	(_____)	= $ _____
11.	Medical	(__ % of Net)	(_____)	= $ _____
12.	Miscellaneous	(__ % of Net)	(_____)	= $ _____
13.	School/ Child Care[2]	(__ % of Net)	(_____)	= $ _____
14.	Investments	(__ % of Net)	(_____)	= $ _____

Total   (Cannot exceed Net Spendable Income) $ _____

15.	Unallocated Surplus Income	(__N/A__)	= $ _____

[1] Refer to Figure 11.1 for percentage guidelines.

[2] Remember this percentage is not included in guideline, and whatever you use must be subtracted from some other category to keep your spending at 100% of NSI.

FORM 3

106

Budget Analysis

GROSS INCOME
PER YEAR _____   NET SPENDABLE INCOME PER MONTH _____

PER MONTH_____

MONTHLY PAYMENT CATEGORY	EXISTING BUDGET	MONTHLY GUIDELINE BUDGET	DIFFERENCE + OR –	NEW MONTHLY BUDGET
1. Tithe				
2. Taxes				
NET SPENDABLE INCOME (PER MONTH)	$_____	$_____	$_____	$_____
3. Housing				
4. Food				
5. Automobile(s)				
6. Insurance				
7. Debts				
8. Enter./Recreation				
9. Clothing				
10. Savings				
11. Medical				
12. Miscellaneous				
13. School/Child Care				
14. Investments				
TOTALS (Items 3 through 14)	$_____	$_____	/////////	$_____
15. Unallocated Surplus Income				

FORM 4

CHAPTER
12
___

STARTING
A BUSINESS

(adapted from *The Pathfinder* by Lee Ellis)

Many people who are unhappy in their jobs, or who are without a job, consider going into business for themselves. Sometimes this is a good option and sometimes it's not. Starting a business can be a complex undertaking, requiring much prayer and consideration, and we could not begin to cover every aspect in this one chapter.

However, we thought it might be helpful to share some of what we have learned from counseling with those who have been both successful and unsuccessful in business start-ups. This chapter will cover some of the key areas and ask some questions that will help you evaluate the wisdom of starting a business.

Also, there are many mothers who would like to start a home business. That's a good way for many women to use their talents to generate some income and still stay at home with their children. Home businesses are generally for supplemental income and usually are much simpler to get going than a full-fledged business. Still, it's important for the home entrepreneurs to know what they are getting into.

Whatever your situation, working through this chapter will introduce you to some of the issues you need to consider before starting a business. Answering the following questions will help you "count the cost" before you begin the building process.

Motivation

As in most other decisions, you should always analyze your motivation for pursuing a course of action. Proper motivation for starting a business might include a strong desire to provide a product or service—a specific talent or idea that could be marketed better by you than by someone else.

Quite often people want to start businesses out of frustration with their current employment situation. That may or may not be a good motivation since, for most people, there are other alternatives. The following questions will help you analyze your motivations.

a. What is your real motivation for considering self-employment? List your reasons in order of priority.

(1)_____

(2)_____

(3)_____

(4)_____

(5)_____

b. What don't you like about your current situation?

_____

c. What alternatives have you considered other than self-employment?

_____

d. What values and needs are not being met in your current situation?

_____

e. Starting a business takes a lot of commitment and hard work. It can be a challenge of enormous magnitude, and it usually takes a burning desire to overcome the obstacles. Is this something you really want and feel strongly led to do?

_____

Knowledge/Experience

Generally we advise that you avoid getting financially involved in things you don't know much about. That principle especially applies to starting a business because it requires an investment of money, time, and energy.

    a. What is your knowledge level about the business you would undertake?

    _____

    b. Do you know what defines a Christian business, and have you studied God's principles for operating a business?

    _____

    NOTE: If not, we recommend you read *Business by the Book* by Larry Burkett.

    c. How much experience do you have in the occupational field you are considering?

    _____

    d. Do you have any business experience (profit and loss responsibility)?

    _____

    e. Have you investigated the government regulations governing the potential business? Are permits or licenses required?

    _____

    f. Are you knowledgeable of the income and Social Security tax requirements that govern self-employed individuals?

    _____

    NOTE: This can be a shock to those who have not had to pay quarterly taxes or self-employment tax.

    g. Do you know how to write a business plan? Have you written a business plan?

    _____

Start-Up Capital

Most businesses fail in the first two years because they are under-capitalized. Before launching into a business, you need to "count the cost" of everything you will need to succeed.

Rather than be too optimistic, plan conservatively regarding income and liberally regarding expenses. A frequent problem is that the business does not generate adequate income to pay overhead and provide a livable income.

Entrepreneurs tend to be too optimistic about how long it will take to develop a business to the point of profitability. Thus they end up living off the money that should be paying the overhead (creditors), and they sink further in debt while trying to hold on until the business takes off.

A common mistake during business start-up is to live by using credit cards. This virtually guarantees a financial disaster and should be avoided.

   a. Where will your start-up and operating capital come from? Do you have enough cash or liquid assets to operate eighteen months to two years without a profit? (That is a good planning figure for how long it will take for most businesses to become profitable.)

   _____

   _____

   _____

   b. Are you considering forming a partnership?

   _____

NOTE: Experience shows that partnerships rarely work out. If you are yoked to someone and that person (or his or her spouse) has different values and motivations than you, you won't be very happy. It's similar to a marriage, except more difficult to maintain. Successful partnerships require both parties to have the mind of Christ (a servant's attitude toward the other partner—with two or more families involved, that rarely occurs).

Financial Records

Quite often those who have an entrepreneurial bent are the very ones who don't enjoy detail work, such as record keeping.

Not having good financial records can cause major problems, because a business owner must make decisions every day, based on how things are going financially. If you don't know where you stand financially, you run a high risk of acting out of ignorance and making a bad (costly) decision.

Keep in mind that the best set of financial records for you will be something you can thoroughly understand. You may have to get some help at first and do some study on your own as well, but the keys to remember are *simplicity* and *timeliness.* Having something that is simple and current is essential for sound financial management. Two such systems are listed later in the Resources section on page 118.

   a. What plans have you made for keeping simple, timely, and accurate financial records?

   _____

   b. Who will be the detail person in your operation? Can you do it? Will your spouse be better suited to this task? Or will you hire someone to assist you?

   _____

   c. If you are not experienced in the use of financial records, such as income statements, balance statements, budgets, and the like, how will you become knowledgeable about these areas?

   _____

Counsel and Information

You'll need information from several sources, but your counsel should come from those who have wisdom, which comes from having a godly perspective toward everything in life. Local Christian business people can be your best source of counsel.

Small Business Development Centers are located in most states and are operated through state universities. They provide help to those who are considering a business start-up, as well as to those who already have a business. Information is usually free or provided at a very low cost.

   a. Have you received adequate counsel regarding the pros and cons of owning your own business?

   _____

   b. Have you developed a list of sources for counsel and information?

   _____

NOTE: The books listed at the end of this chapter contain excellent resource lists.

Personnel

The simplest business by far is a one-person operation in which the owner *is* the business. However, many situations will require additional employees. The minute you hire one person, the situation changes considerably because many laws and rules apply that complicate the workload. You need to be familiar with withholding taxes, FICA, the Fair Labor Employment Act, OSHA, worker's compensation, and many other areas.

Also, in any business, getting the right person is so important. Hiring the wrong person is one of the worst things that can happen to a small businessperson. Develop a written job description and criteria for the job before you start looking for the person.

As you look for your personnel, keep in mind the principles you have learned in this workbook about matching the person to the job. The same concepts apply. If you know the pattern of what it will take to do the job, then you can look for a person with that pattern when hiring.

Generally, an entrepreneur's first hire should be someone who is opposite from him or her. If you are a big-picture person, you will likely need a detailed person to follow through on day-to-day activities and record keeping.

Conversely, if you are a detailed person, you likely will need an outgoing, enterprising person to promote the business. Study the personality section in Chapter 3 as you think through the type of person you want to hire.

a. Are you familiar with the rules and regulations that apply to employees?

_____

b. Have you developed a written job description for the opening you want to fill?

_____

c. Have you given consideration to the pattern of the person you want to hire?

_____

Skills and Abilities _____   Vocational Interests _____

Work Values _____   Personality _____

Timing a Business Start-Up

As in any other endeavor, timing can be of the utmost importance. Good timing applies to you in your personal situation, and it applies to the product and services you offer.

a. Is the endeavor compatible with your life and other responsibilities at this time? Has the window of opportunity closed, has it just opened, or will it not open until some future date?

_____

b. Is the timing right for this particular product or service?

_____

This is really a marketing question that will probably require some careful thought, advice, and research.

Personality

Generally entrepreneurs tend to operate from a confident, results-oriented, problem-solver, and challenge-oriented (Dominant) personality style. They are usually big-picture visionaries who believe they can overcome any obstacles that arise. There are, however, good examples of every personality style being effective as business leaders.

Entrepreneurs generally step out on their own because they don't like to work for someone else. They want to be in charge. They are generally bold and willing to take risks; sometimes they succeed and sometimes they fail. True entrepreneurs are very competitive and prefer to work rather than to relax.

The secret is to know your strengths and weaknesses and work within them, conforming to the situation as necessary. You should be aware, however, that any time you compromise for an extended period of time, stress results. If you have high needs for stability and security, you may not want the risks of being an entrepreneur.

On the other hand, the business you are considering may not be high risk. For instance, going on your own in an appliance repair business would be quite different from marketing a new product. You should understand your personality and give this area high priority in your decision to start a business.

Is your personality suited to owning and operating your own business? Compare your strengths from Chapter 3.

Time-Energy-Family

A realistic evaluation of the time commitment required to start and operate a business is essential. Solving one problem after another will require energy—physical energy and emotional energy that comes from your drive and enthusiasm to see a project completed. A business start-up can be a consuming experience, and frequently marriages and families suffer even to the point of breakup. Consider these questions in this area.

a. Do you understand the time commitment required to see this undertaking through successfully?

_____

b. Are you a high energy person? Is your enthusiasm so high that your work will seem like play?

_____

c. How will the business affect your relationship with your spouse?

_____

d. How will the business affect your relationship with your children? Will you be able to spend quantity time with your family, as well as quality time?

_____

e. How will your business endeavors affect your relationship with the Lord?

_____

God's Will

Go back to the first section on motivation in this chapter. Consider your true motivations for pursuing this course of action in light of what you believe God would have you do.

a. Have you truly sought God's will in this decision?

_____

b. Will this decision enable you to better glorify the Lord in your work?

_____

c. Do you and your spouse both have a peace in the decision that this is truly God's will for your life?

_____

Conclusion

We've taken you through the above issues because they cover the main problems we have found in the "Hall of Horrors" museum of common mistakes made when starting a business. It is not intended to discourage you but to assist you in making a good decision.

Remember, every situation is different, so every issue discussed above won't apply with the same significance. If you are going to sell homemade pies to your friends and neighbors, your situation is fairly simple, but if you expand into a small baking operation employing several people, the requirements will be quite different.

We can't emphasize enough the importance of prayerful and patient consideration in making a decision to start a business. Do your homework and let the Lord guide you into His will.

Resources

Books

Business by the Book, Larry Burkett. Nashville, TN:
    Thomas Nelson, 1990.
Home Business 101, Sharon Carr. Tarrytown, NY:
    Fleming H. Revell Company, 1989.
Homemade Business, Donna Partow. Colorado Springs, CO:
    Focus on the Family, 1992.
    Contains an excellent resource section for any new business.
Working at Home, Lindsey O'Connor. Eugene, OR: Harvest House, 1990.

Newsletters

Money Matters A monthly Christian economic newsletter
    601 Broad St SE, Gainesville, GA 30501
    From Larry Burkett and Christian Financial Concepts

Christian Organizations Supporting Business Leaders

Biblical Leadership for Excellence
    6219 Moccasin St, San Antonio, TX 78230, (210)342-3340
    Management training organization designed to train business leaders to incorporate God's standards for excellence in their careers.
Christian Businessmen's Committee of the USA
    1800 McCallie Ave, Chattanooga, TN 37404, (423)698-4444 or (800) 566-2262
    This organization's purpose is to assist businessmen and women in operating their companies according to God's principles and sharing the gospel of Jesus Christ through their businesses.
Christian Financial Concepts, Inc
    601 Broad St SE, Gainesville, GA 30501, (770)534-1000
    Business seminars given by qualified instructors throughout the United States. A business seminar schedule is available upon request.
Fellowship of Companies for Christ
    4201 N Peachtree Rd Ste 200, Atlanta, GA 30341, (770)457-9700 or (800) 664-3224
    This is a membership organization that conducts various business seminars for its members.
Turn Around, Inc
    601 Broad St SE, Gainesville, GA 30501, (770)534-1000
    This ministry counsels people who are facing or have already filed for bankruptcy.

Record Keeping Systems

McBee Systems
> 299 Cherry Hill Rd, Parsippany, NJ 07054-1175, (973)263-3225 or (800) 526-1272
> This organization may be contacted for information on setting up a business bookkeeping system.

Safeguard Business Systems
> 455 Maryland Dr, PO Box 7501, Fort Washington, PA 19034, (800)523-2422
> This organization may be contacted for information on setting up a business bookkeeping system.

Tape Series

*"God's Principles for Operating a Business," Larry Burkett, Gainesville, GA: Christian Financial Concepts
> (11 cassettes, 1 outline).

*Can be purchased from Christian Financial Concepts materials department (800) 722-1976 or Web site www.cfcministry.org.

Internet Sites

Christian Entrepreneur Online (CEO)—founded to encourage Christians in the business arena to promote application of biblical principles and practices in daily business activities and to provide tools that integrate a biblical perspective with daily business issues.
http://www.tceonline.com//

Service Corps of Retired Executives (SCORE)—a resource partner with the U.S. Small Business Administration, dedicated to aiding in the formation, growth, and success of small business nationwide.
http://www.score.org/rightframe.html

Let's Talk Business Network, Inc. [LTB]—founded by entrepreneurs to provide twenty-first century guidance and support for entrepreneurs and emerging growth companies.
http://www.audionet.com/shows/ltbn/

Center for Entrepreneurial Leadership Clearinghouse on Entrepreneurship Education—a large database containing abstracts from research articles on entrepreneurship.
http://www.celcee.edu/

Entrepreneur Magazine—a Web site from the editors of *Entrepreneur magazine.*
http://www.entrepreneurmag.com/smbiz_links_smbiz.hts

Inc. Magazine Online—a Web site from the editors of *Inc.* magazine.
http://www.inc.com/

Your Small Office—a Web site from the editors of *Small Office Computing* and *Home Office Computing*.
http://www.smalloffice.com/

More Financial Resources from Moody Press and Larry Burkett.

Debt Free-Living
How To Get Out of Debt...and Stay Out!

Proven strategies, coupled with God's principles of finance, give you a plan for successful money management. Burkett offers solid, biblically sound advice for all ages and income levels. **More than 260,000 in print.**

ISBN: 0-8024-2565-8 Paperback, Finances

How to Manage Your Money
An In-Depth Bible Study on Personal Finances

This newly re-packaged bestseller contains updated material, plus a step-by-step, in-depth study of God's principles for money management. **More than 700,000 sold.**

ISBN: 0-8024-1476-1, Paperback, Finances

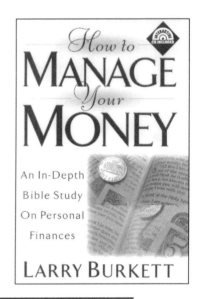

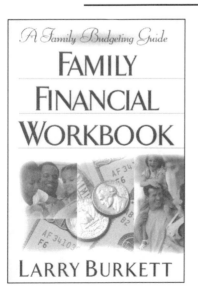

Family Financial Workbook
A Family Budgeting Guide

Includes every easy-to-follow worksheet you need to structure and maintain your family's budget. Contains extra worksheets so you can go back year after year. Features NEW interactive CD-ROM containing a helpful, systematic, interactive budget guide. **More than 600,000 sold as *The Financial Planning Workbook*.**

ISBN: 0-8024-1475-3, Paperback, Finances

The World's Easiest Pocket Guides

Most people fail to learn the basics of holding down a full-time job, paying bills, renting an apartment, using a credit card, and saving money, and are woefully unprepared for life in the real world when they move out on their own.

Larry Burkett gives the reader sound advice from a godly, biblical perspective. In *Your First Full-Time Job, Your First Savings Plan, Your First Investment,* and *Your First Financial Plan,* Larry walks you step-by-step through finding and keeping a job, saving money, investing money without losing your shirt, and getting and maintaining control of your money.

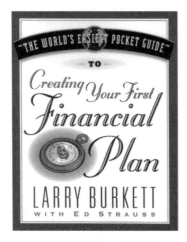

ISBN: 0-8024-0994-6, Paperback, Finances

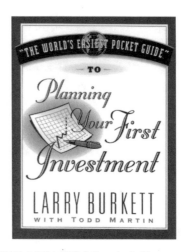

ISBN: 0-8024-0993-8, Paperback, Finances

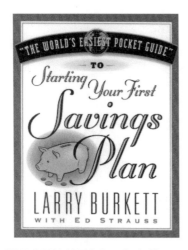

ISBN: 0-8024-0996-2, Paperback, Finances

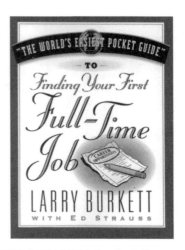

ISBN: 0-8024-0995-4, Paperback, Finances

More From Best-Selling Authors
Gary Chapman & Larry Burkett --
The World's <u>Easiest</u> Guides!

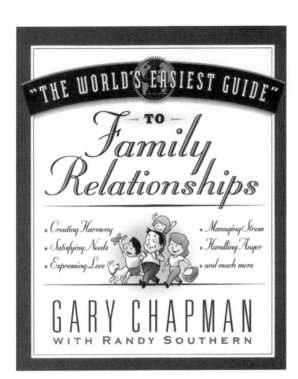

"The World's Easiest Guide" *to Family Relationships*

From the author of Five Love Languages, Gary Chapman has gathered the most treasured insights from his previous books -- *Five Love Languages, Loving Solutions, Five Signs of a Loving Family, The Other Side of Love,* and *Toward a Growing Marriage* to name a few -- to create an easy and comprehensive guide to family relationships.

ISBN: 1-881273-40-7, Paperback, Family

"The World's Easiest Guide" *to Finances*

The Leading Christian financial expert Larry Burkett answers the call for a simplified, yet comprehensive guide to financial management with *The World's Easiest Guide to Finances.* This guide makes complicated terms and concepts easy to grasp with a touch of humor, and builds the confidence of all readers that they can understand and implement the information.

ISBN: 1-881273-38-5, Paperback, Finances

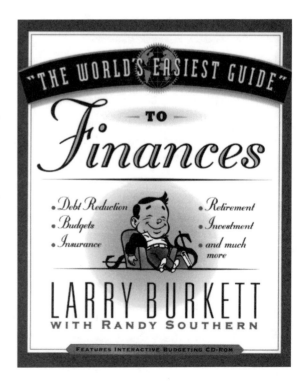